PRIVATE LANDLORDS AND HOUSING BENEFIT

Mark Bevan
Peter A Kemp
David Rhodes

RESEARCH REPORT

CENTRE FOR HOUSING POLICY
University of York

Published by:
Centre for Housing Policy
University of York
York YO1 5DD
Telephone 01904 433691
Fax 01904 432318

ISBN 1 874797 71 4

Typeset by Joanne Gatenby in the Centre for Housing Policy
Printed by York Publishing Service

The **Joseph Rowntree Foundation** has supported this project as part of its programme of research and innovative development projects, which it hopes will be of value to policy makers and practitioners. The facts presented and views expressed in this report however, are those of the authors and not necessarily those of the Foundation.

Acknowledgements

We would like to thank the landlords and agents who agreed to be interviewed for this research; without their help, the study could not have been carried out. We are grateful to the Joseph Rowntree Foundation who funded the work and to our project advisory group, who gave up their time to provide us with very helpful support, advice and feedback. Joanne Gatenby and Jane Allen were responsible for the production of the report. Responsibility for the contents rests solely with the authors.

The authors

Mark Bevan is a research assistant and David Rhodes is a research fellow in the Centre for Housing Policy. Peter Kemp currently holds the Joseph Rowntree Chair of Housing Policy and is Director of the Centre for Housing Policy at the University of York; in January 1996 he returns to Glasgow University to take up a newly established Chair in Housing and Urban Studies.

Contents

List of tables

Chapter One
Introduction

The sharp increase in the average private sector rent and the rising cost of Housing Benefit since 1989 have led to concerns about landlords taking advantage of Housing Benefit. This concern has focused on the letting strategies and rent setting behaviour of private landlords which, it is claimed, have been distorted by the Housing Benefit scheme.

In the light of these developments, the Government has put forward measures to be introduced in January 1996 for reforming Housing Benefit (DSS, 1995) which are aimed at preventing it from being paid on high rents and at giving tenants an incentive both to shop around for accommodation and to bargain with the landlord over the rent to be paid (Lilley, 1994).

The controversy which has surrounded these issues has generated a great deal of heat but relatively little light. Much of the argument seems to be based on media reports and on anecdote rather than on research evidence. The aim of this report, therefore, is to examine landlord's rent setting behaviour and letting strategies with respect to Housing Benefit in order to inform the debate and provide a sounder basis on which to develop policy.

Setting rents

It has been argued that landlords are charging people on Housing Benefit an artificially high rent. Indeed, one politician is reported to have claimed that private landlords could virtually set any rent they wished and have it paid by the state. As a result, they were 'costing taxpayers billions' of pounds (see Timmins, 1994) and 'getting fat' on Housing Benefit.

Such claims, at least in their most extreme form, appear to misunderstand or take no account of how the Housing Benefit scheme works. With certain specified exceptions, local authorities are not allowed to pay Housing Benefit on rents that are unreasonably high or on accommodation that is unreasonably large. Instead, they are required to restrict the level of rent that is eligible to be taken into account for Housing Benefit purposes to an amount that is reasonable. Moreover, the arrangements for the subsidy which local authorities receive from central government to reimburse them for their Housing Benefit expenditure have incentives that are designed to encourage local authorities to use their power to restrict unreasonably high rents.

These subsidy incentives operate via the rent officer referral system. Under the arrangements in place prior to the January 1996 changes, when a private tenant applies for Housing Benefit, the claim is referred to the local rent officer service to make a determination of rent for that accommodation. Rent officers are required to determine whether or not (1) the rent is above the market level or (2) exceptionally high, or (3) the accommodation is unreasonably large taking into account the size and composition of the claimant's household.

If the accommodation is *over the market value*, the rent officer has to determine what would be a reasonable market rent for the property; this is defined as the rent which someone not on Housing Benefit would pay for the accommodation. If the rent is *exceptionally high*, the rent officer has to determine what would be the 'highest reasonable rent' that would not be exceptionally high for that accommodation; the aim being to prevent Housing Benefit subsidy being paid on 'top end of the market' properties. Finally, if the accommodation is *over large*, the rent officer has to determine a notional market rent for similar accommodation that is not over large for the claimant's needs.

These rent officer determinations function as the subsidy ceiling for Housing Benefit purposes. Under the present arrangements, local authorities normally receive subsidy from central government at a rate of 95 per cent on rent up to the rent officer's determination, but nil on benefit paid on rent in excess of the determination. In the case of certain vulnerable groups, local authorities receive 60 per cent subsidy on Housing Benefit paid in excess of the rent officer's determination.

As a result, local authorities have a strong financial incentive to restrict the eligible rent to the rent officer's determination. These determinations are also intended to act as guidance to local authorities about what is a reasonable rent for the accommodation, though they are required to investigate the circumstances of each claim. In fact, research has found that local authorities generally do use the rent officer's determination in the great majority of cases as the eligible rent for Housing Benefit purposes (Kemp and McLaverty, 1993a).

While extreme claims about landlords 'getting fat' on Housing Benefit ignore or misunderstand how the scheme works, this does not mean that there is no case at all to be answered. This case derives at least in part from the fact that Housing Benefit can cover all of the eligible rent for *some* claimants (mainly those on Income Support) and that, for *all* claimants, it covers all of any reasonable increase in the level of their rent.

Thus Housing Benefit recipients, irrespective of whether they receive full or partial Housing Benefit, are fully insulated from any increase or decrease in the rent.

During the financial year 1993/94, in 43 per cent of cases, rent officers made a determination that was lower than the contractual rent initially agreed between landlord and tenant. In 33 per cent of referrals (that is, 67% of reduced rent cases) the reduction was made because the rent, in the rent officer's judgement, was over the market value (DoE, 1995).

Assuming that rent officers are making accurate assessments of the reasonable market rent, this implies that in a substantial minority of cases, landlords are agreeing rents with their tenants that are more than someone not on Housing Benefit would pay for the accommodation.

This raises the questions of how it is that some landlords are apparently charging (at least initially) tenants on Housing Benefit a higher rent than rent officers believe is the reasonable market rent for the accommodation? Is it a deliberate attempt to take advantage of the Housing Benefit scheme? Or is it because landlords do not know what they can charge for accommodation? There is no readily available and reliable rent index[1] for the private residential sector and this may be one cause of the apparent over charging, particularly in respect of informal landlords and those not operating on a commercial or long term basis.

Alternatively, it could be argued that landlords will require a risk premium to let accommodation to people on Housing Benefit because of the increased costs and risks that they may face as a result of letting to this client group. If so, then the market rent for tenants on Housing Benefit would be higher than for less risky client groups, though the rules governing rent officer determinations take no account of this risk factor.

Although the eligible rent may be restricted for Housing Benefit purposes, this is not necessarily the amount which the landlord is charging the tenant. One way in which tenants may respond to the eligible rent being restricted for Housing Benefit is to try to negotiate a lower contractual rent with the landlord. A recent study of six local authorities in England and Wales found that, among tenants who had not moved on by the time of the survey, a quarter of tenants whose rent had been restricted during the previous year had managed to negotiate a lower rent with the landlord (Kemp and McLaverty, 1995).

This raises questions about whether landlords are aware of, or understand, the role of the rent officer or the rules governing unreasonable rents in the Housing Benefit scheme; how

---

[1]   The Joseph Rowntree Foundation is currently funding the production of an index of private rents, yields and capital values at the Centre for Housing Policy, University of York.

they decide upon what rent to charge and whether they take the rent officer into account when doing so; and whether they are prepared to negotiate the rent with a tenant whose rent has been restricted for Housing Benefit purposes.

Letting preferences

A related issue is whether the Housing Benefit system has affected landlord's letting strategies. First of all, there is the question of whether landlords prefer, or deliberately seek, to let their accommodation to people on Housing Benefit.

If it is true that landlords can somehow manage to charge people on Housing Benefit a higher rent than they can non-recipients, then - other things being equal - they may be more likely to let their accommodation to recipients than would otherwise be the case.

However, other things are not necessarily equal. As suggested above, there may well be greater risks facing a landlord letting to someone on Housing Benefit than someone not on benefit. For example, Housing Benefit can take weeks or in some cases even months to be processed, during which time the tenant may be forced to run up rent arrears, as a recent study of private tenants has found (Kemp and McLaverty, 1995).

Again, even when the Housing Benefit does finally come through, the tenant may find that the eligible rent has been restricted and that he or she cannot in the event afford to pay the full rent. As a result, the tenant may not be able repay the rent arrears in full or may seek to negotiate a lower rent than that originally agreed with the landlord (Kemp et al, 1994). Either way, the landlord may end up with less rental income than they had anticipated.

For these and other reasons landlords may decide that it is too risky, or at least less preferable, to let accommodation to people on Housing Benefit.

On the other hand, for some landlords, letting to people on Housing Benefit may be more attractive than to other types of tenant because of the prospect of getting the benefit paid direct to them rather than to the tenant. Once the tenant's Housing Benefit application has been processed, if they have agreed to the benefit being paid direct to the landlord, the rent (or at least that part of it covered by Housing Benefit) is virtually a guaranteed income.

This raises the question of whether landlords do in fact see Housing Benefit paid direct to them as a form of rent guarantee. If they do, then this might reduce any risk premium that landlords require for letting to people on Housing Benefit.

Secondly, there is the question of whether landlords have sought to target particular groups of tenants, such as the vulnerable groups, as a result of the pre-January 1996 rules governing the Housing Benefit scheme. Under these rules, local authorities are required to pay Housing Benefit on rent that is over the market value if the household falls in to one of the protected vulnerable groups, unless (a) there is suitable alternative accommodation and (b) it is reasonable to expect the claimant to move. It is sometimes suggested that, for this reason, landlords are targeting vulnerable group claimants such as lone parents in order to obtain above market rents (DSS, 1995). Hence one of the aims of the research reported here was to examine whether landlords target particular types of tenant, such as lone parents or the other vulnerable groups.

New arrangements

The changes to Housing Benefit which are to be implemented from January 1996 may have an important bearing on landlord's rent setting and letting strategies.

Under the new arrangements[2] - which essentially apply to claims made after 1 January 1996 - Housing Benefit will be assessed on the full eligible rent (subject to the rules regarding reasonableness outlined above) up to what is referred to as the 'local reference rent' for the locality. On the excess above the local reference rent, Housing Benefit will be assessed on only half of the difference between the (reasonable) 'property specific rent' and the local reference rent.

As a result, the marginal rate of benefit will be 100 per cent up to the local reference rent but only 50 per cent on the excess over that amount. The Government hopes that this change will give private tenants on Housing Benefit a financial incentive to shop around for cheap accommodation and to bargain with prospective landlords over the rent to be charged.

The local reference rent will be determined by the rent officer service. It will be calculated 'by determining the mid-point of a range of rents for similar accommodation in the locality' (DSS, 1995, p4). This range will exclude exceptionally high or low rents. The 'locality' will be decided by the rent officer in the light of the relevant local property market context.

Local authorities will have the power to request a redetermination of the local reference rent where they believe the rent officer to be in error, as they currently do on individual properties referred to them under the current arrangements. However, tenants are to be

---

[2]   See Zebedee and Ward (1995) for a more detailed exposition of the new arrangements.

given a new right to request the local authority to seek a redetermination on their behalf, of either their own property specific rent or the local reference rent.

The rules on vulnerable groups are to be scrapped. Instead, local authorities will have the discretion to pay Housing Benefit on rent above the maximum eligible rent (but not above the contractual rent) in exceptional circumstances, subject to a permitted total level of expenditure.

Finally, a procedure called pre-tenancy determinations (PTDs) - which had been proposed by the Institute of Rent Officers (1992) and supported by others (eg Kemp and McLaverty, 1993b) - is to be introduced. The purpose of PTDs is to give prospective tenants and landlords an indication of the likely rent (the property specific rent) that will be eligible for Housing Benefit. Previous research has shown that uncertainty about what rent would be acceptable for Housing Benefit is a major source of anxiety for private tenants who are moving while on benefit (Kemp, et al, 1994; Kemp and McLaverty, 1995). This new arrangement should help to reduce the uncertainty and hence the anxiety for private tenants who are moving whilst on Housing Benefit, but what do landlords think about the idea?

Aims of the research

The aims of the research were:

▶   to examine landlords' knowledge and understanding of the role of the rent officers and the rules governing unreasonable rents in the Housing Benefit scheme

▶   to examine landlords' attitudes to restrictions in their tenants' eligible rent for Housing Benefit purposes; and

▶   to investigate the impact of Housing Benefit, including rent restrictions, on landlords' (a) rent setting behaviour and (b) their letting strategies.

In examining these questions, the research was also able to address several important policy innovations which were being debated at the time of the fieldwork. These included the idea of introducing rent ceilings on Housing Benefit and the proposal for pre-tenancy determinations. PTD are included in the package of changes to be introduced into the Housing Benefit scheme in January 1996. However, although discussed in the media, rent celings were not in the event part of the package of changes. Instead, local reference rents - which act as a threshold affecting the rate of benefit, rather than as a ceiling - are to be introduced Although the precise details of the proposals were not available at the time of the fieldwork, we were able to elicit landlords' views on the broad concepts of rent ceilings and PTDs.

In addition, we were also able to examine landlords' attitudes to the proposal made by the Government (DoE, 1994) that greater use should be made of the private rented sector to house people accepted by local authorities for rehousing on the grounds of homelessness. One of the criticisms that has been levelled against this proposal is that rent levels (and hence Housing Benefit costs) are higher in the privately rented sector compared with social housing (LHU, 1994). But quite apart from rent levels and Housing Benefit costs, the important question remains as to whether landlords would be willing to let their accommodation to homeless households accepted for rehousing by local authorities.

Methods

Semi-structured qualitative interviews were carried out with 47 landlords and letting agents between October and December 1994. The interviews were conducted in the five case study areas of London, Birmingham, Cardiff, Sunderland and Manchester.

The sample of landlords was drawn from an earlier survey of private tenants whose rent had been restricted for Housing Benefit purposes (Kemp and McLaverty, 1995). These tenants were asked if they would be willing for their landlords to be interviewed, and where they were, their landlords' contact details were recorded.

In addition, a telephone survey was completed with 46 of these 47 landlords, the details and results of which are set out and explained in the Appendix.

Structure of the report

Landlords' letting and rent setting strategies as well as their attitudes towards Housing Benefit are best understood, not in isolation, but in the context of their motivations and behaviour as landlords more generally. For this reason, while focusing especially on Housing Benefit, tenant selection and rent setting, the report examines the wider aspects of private landlordism as well.

Chapter two presents a typology of the landlords interviewed. The characteristics of landlords and their motivations for letting are also described.

In chapter three, the respondents' feelings about being a landlord are considered. This focuses upon how landlords feel they are viewed, what they see as the positive and negative things about being a landlord, and their expectations and intentions.

Chapter four looks at respondents' experiences of managing their property. It examines their use of letting agents, how tenants are found, and rent in advance and deposits. Landlords' attitudes towards rent guarantees, the tenancy agreements that they use, how they deal with rent arrears, and their experience of evictions and the courts are also explored.

In chapter five, the letting strategies of landlords are considered. This examines their preferred types of tenant, how they would define the ideal tenant', and how they go about selecting tenants. It also looks at their views on rent ceilings and pre-tenancy determinations, and their attitudes towards accepting homeless households on behalf of local authorities.

Chapter six investigates landlords' experiences of Housing Benefit. It focuses on the time taken to process claims, the issue of tenants moving out before a claim has been processed, the payment of Housing Benefit direct to the landlord, the recovery of overpayments where the benefit is paid direct to the landlord, and landlords' experience of dealing with local authority Housing Benefit offices.

Chapter seven focuses on rent setting. This explores the attitudes of landlords towards negotiating the rent, rent setting and Housing Benefit and also examines the awareness, experiences and views of landlords towards rent restrictions.

The final chapter summarises the main findings of the research in relation to Housing Benefit and sets out some conclusions.

Housing Benefit and 'unreasonable' rents

The research findings presented in this report form part of a linked series of projects, funded by the Joseph Rowntree Foundation, which have examined different aspects of the relationship between Housing Benefit and 'unreasonable' rents in the privately rent sector.

The first study examined how local authorities make decisions about the reasonableness of rents and accommodation in making determinations of Housing Benefit entitlement (Kemp and McLaverty, 1993a); it also looked at the role of the rent officer service in this process and how they implement their duties in the Housing Benefit scheme (Kemp and McLaverty,1993b).

The second study looked at the extent to which, in moving house, private tenants are influenced by the fact that they were on Housing Benefit and at how they respond to having their rent restricted for Housing Benefit purposes (Kemp and McLaverty, 1995).

The third study, reported here, has examined the extent to which landlords' letting strategies and rent setting behaviour are affected by Housing Benefit.

A paper drawing together the findings from these three studies and setting out options for policy, is expected to be published by the Joseph Rowntree Foundation in due course.

Chapter Two
The Landlords

Introduction

The aim of this chapter is to describe the respondents who were interviewed. Using this information, a typology of landlords is set out, and this will be used as a basis for discussion throughout the remainder of the report.

The chapter begins by looking at the different types of respondents, and how they have been classified. Next, there is an examination of some of the basic characteristics of the respondents, including who they were, how they became involved in letting, and details of their portfolios. The third section of the chapter analyses the respondents' motivations for letting. This discussion includes an examination of why they became landlords, the importance of rental income and capital gains, and the impact of the property slump. The final part of the chapter is a summary of the main findings.

Types of respondent

A clear finding to emerge from the research is that the landlords were not an homogeneous group. In simple terms, the 47 qualitative interviews were conducted with two types of respondents: landlords and letting agents. However, within these basic groupings there was a diversity of business arrangements, which included managing agents, private individuals, partnership landlords, company landlords, and respondents who were both a managing agent and a landlord (Table 2.1).

In their survey of private landlords, Thomas and Snape (1995) classified the landlords they interviewed into three main types: sideline landlords, business landlords and organisational landlords. Whilst our categorisation is not based on exactly the same criteria as that of Thomas and Snape, we have borrowed the labels of 'sideline landlords' and 'business landlords', as these terms usefully describe the landlords interviewed in this survey.

Table 2.1
Business arrangements of the respondents

Business type	Number
Private individual landlords	34
Partnership landlord	1
Company landlord	1
Managing agents	9
Managing agent and landlord	2
Total	47

Although there was a diversity of respondents, it was possible to broadly identify three main types in terms of their motivations, how they viewed their portfolio or lettings, and their basic characteristics. There were 11 *managing agents*, seven *business landlords,* and 29 *sideline landlords*. *Business landlords* were full-time landlords for whom letting property was their primary source of income. *Sideline landlords*, on the other hand, were not primarily occupied as landlords, but were part-time landlords who were letting as a sideline to something else. However, it was also apparent that there was a divide amongst the sideline landlords: one sub-group had a more formal and considered approach to their roles as landlords than the other. These two sub-groups are respectively referred to as *formal sideline landlords*, and *informal sideline landlords*. The *formal sideline landlords* had an organised approach to letting, either relying on letting agents or using assured shorthold tenancies. Their lettings were often viewed as an investment for the future. This type of landlord generally had an awareness of the 1988 Housing Act and the procedures associated with the payment of Housing Benefit. In comparison, *informal sideline landlords* were letting in a very casual manner without formalised agreements. They tended not to think of themselves as being landlords, and viewed their tenants either as friends or as part of their family. In addition, most of them viewed the property they were letting primarily as their home. They were unaware of their rights as landlords, and had little understanding of the Housing Benefit system. Table 2.2 provides a summary of the different types of respondent.

Key features of the respondent types

The *managing agents* were the most clearly defined group of respondents. Their involvement was generally one of performing a lettings and complete   management service on behalf of their landlords. The agents would less frequently be required to only provide a lettings service (finding tenants and organising tenancy agreements) for landlords who wished to carry out the day to day management themselves. The fees they charged, which were usually a fixed proportion of the rent, varied depending on whether they provided the full management service or just the lettings service.

Table 2.2
Types of respondent

Respondent type	Number
Managing agents	11
Business landlords	7
Sideline landlords:	29
Formal	17
Informal	12
Total	47

A caveat to the classification of the landlords is that the distinctions between the different types of landlords, whilst being generally identifiable, were occasionally blurred. This situation was partly the result of unusual cases with regard to certain characteristics (size of portfolio, for example), but also because there was a small number of landlords who were transitional; a feature of particular relevance to some of the formal sideline landlords who were becoming business oriented in their approaches. However, as a general rule it was possible to discern the different types of landlords, and consider their specific features where relevant.

The most clearly demarcated type of *landlords* were the *business landlords*: they were full-time private individual landlords. Their motivation for becoming landlords was that they saw the business as a good way to make a living. Reflecting this attitude, these landlords typically had more lettings than the sideline landlords, and they valued their portfolio mainly for their current rental income rather than for future capital gains. It was typical for this type of landlord to have built up their portfolios over a number of years through a process of reinvestment, sometimes having been originally involved on a part-time basis whilst in other employment (that is, they had originally been sideline landlords).

As the term implies, *sideline landlords* were not full-time landlords, but were principally involved in some other activity - usually full-time paid employment. The more *formally operating sideline landlords* were typically non-resident private individuals who had lettings at one or two properties. The main reason why this type of landlord had initially become involved in letting was because they had been unable to sell due to the slump in the owner occupied market. Some still intended to sell if prices improved, but others had found letting a useful way to earn extra income. Many of this type of landlord viewed their property for security in the future, and especially for when they were retired: in this sense the importance of rental income would change from the need to cover their current costs of their mortgages to providing an income in the future.

The *informally operating sideline landlords* were usually simply letting out one room in their own homes. Many of these respondents did not consider themselves to be landlords at all; and many had not actively sought tenants, but were simply helping out a friend or a member of their family. It was common for this type of landlord to view their lodger as a friend, or, even though they were not related, as a member of their family. Those who had actively sought tenants had invariably done so to gain rental income to contribute towards their mortgage repayments. This type of landlord frequently saw their letting activity as a temporary phase in their lives, either expecting to sell their homes if house prices improved, or not taking in another lodger when their current one had left.

To help clarify these distinctions between the different types of respondents, a brief outline of a typical respondent from each group is given below. The rest of the chapter will deal with the issues in more depth.

A typical managing agent

This respondent was a managing agent and also an estate agent. The estate agency began operating in 1990, but diversified into handling lettings, which was seen as a linked business, shortly afterwards. The motivation for starting up a lettings side to the business was due to the decreasing number of sales they were experiencing as a result of the slump in the owner occupied housing market. Three quarters of the company's business was now in lettings, and the remainder was in residential sales. They managed between 70 and 80 properties of a range of types, with both shared and sole occupancy.

The agency said that they operated on behalf of a range of landlord types, some of whom were investment oriented and expected a rate of return on rental income, some wanted the costs of their mortgages covered until they were able to sell, and others were letting properties they had inherited. No matter which type of landlord they were acting for, however, they set rents according to the market.

The agency acquired their portfolio from three main sources: advertising; recommendations from existing client landlords; and from people coming to them to sell, but being unable to do so. The lettings side of the business was viewed as being the most important part of their work, as it accounted for the majority of their trade. The effect of the property slump was that they believed they had an increase in lettings from landlords trapped in negative equity.

A typical business landlord

This respondent was a non-resident private individual landlord, who had been letting property for 20 years. His portfolio consisted of ten properties, which had been converted into a total of 27 lettings. One house comprised five bedsits, whilst the rest of the properties accommodated tenants in self-contained two or three bedroom flats.

Quite typically for this group of landlords, the portfolio had been built up over a number of years by a continual process of reinvestment. Whereas the landlord had originally been involved in letting as a sideline to employment, he was now a full-time landlord who viewed his portfolio as an investment for rental income. Capital gains was not a prime consideration.

This individual gave two reasons for becoming a landlord: he believed that accommodation was a basic requirement and, therefore, that there would always be a demand for rented homes; and secondly, his employment in the printing industry had become increasingly insecure, thus motivating him to concentrate on developing his lettings business.

Whilst being currently unsure what rate of return he was achieving on rental income, it had been calculated to be six per cent in the past. The landlord thought that his current rate of return would be higher than six per cent, but that this was due to falling property values rather than increases in rent levels. At the same time, however, the landlord believed that another effect of the property slump was to make more property available for renting. The result of this increase was that tenants now had more freedom to shop around, and this had impacted on the amount of rent he was able to charge.

A typical formal sideline landlord

This respondent owned three properties which he had converted into self-contained flats. Initially, the landlord had been forced into letting because he had been unable to sell due to the depressed prices on the owner occupied market, but had subsequently found that he enjoyed letting property. As a builder, it was easy for him to buy cheap properties, renovate them and convert them into flats.

The importance of rental income primarily lay in covering the outgoings on his property, and to a lesser extent as a way of accumulating savings with which to acquire more property to let. The landlord now viewed his portfolio as a long-term investment, possibly to be handed down to his sons, and also as security for his family in case anything happened to him. The slump in the owner occupied housing market was now viewed in a positive way by the landlord, as it made more cheap properties available for purchase.

A typical informal sideline landlord

This respondent was a resident private individual landlord. She was letting one room in her home, and sharing the use of her kitchen, bathroom and living room with her tenant. The landlord had begun letting in 1991, and had never let before. The landlord started to let because she was having difficulties meeting her mortgage repayments - ideally she would prefer not to let at all.

The rental income was used to help pay the mortgage, and cover the additional costs incurred from having a lodger. In this respect, rental income was very important to the landlord, but had not been considered in terms of a rate of return.

Background details

Whilst the majority of the landlords (24) were not living at the property they were letting, a large minority (12) were resident at their address (or one of their addresses). None of the *business landlords* were resident landlords. Amongst the *sideline landlords* there were clear differences between the two sub-groups: almost all the *formal sideline landlords* were not resident (only two were), whereas nearly all the *informal sideline landlords* were resident landlords (only two were not).

The *managing agents* were operating their businesses in a full-time manner, as would be expected; and the same was also the case for the *business landlords*, for whom being a landlord was their sole and full-time occupation. In comparison, *sideline landlords* were part-time landlords, with their role as landlords being one of accompaniment to some other, usually predominant, activity. Most commonly, *sideline landlords* were in employment, and this was especially the case for the *formal sideline landlords* (one landlord was retired, and the rest were employed). The *informal landlords* also saw themselves not primarily as landlords, as letting was ancillary to something else. Indeed, several of these landlords did not consider themselves to be landlords at all, often seeing their role as simply temporarily helping someone out. This group of landlords was, however, less likely to be in employment than the more formally operating   sideline landlords: two were unemployed, two were students, and one was retired (the others were in employment).

When became involved in letting

Landlords had started letting as long ago as 1953, and as recently as 1993 (about one year before the interview). Typically, a landlord would have started letting during the 1980s. However, the general trend was that the more informal the landlord, the more likely they were to have started letting in or after 1989, after the introduction of the 1988 Housing Act. This finding does not necessarily imply, however, that the 1988 Act was influential in encouraging lettings activity, as will be discussed under 'motivations' below.

The *informal sideline landlords* were the most likely to have started letting after the introduction of the 1988 Act: seven of these landlords who stated when they began letting, had done so in 1989 or later, compared with four who had started letting before then. The *informal landlords* were also those who had been letting the longest - one had begun letting in 1953 and one in 1954. Slightly more of the *formal sideline landlords* had started letting before the 1988 Act than had started after its introduction (nine compared with seven).

With one exception, the *business landlords* had started letting prior to the introduction of the 1988 Act. The business landlord who was the exception to this rule had started letting in 1989, and considered the Act to be an extremely influential factor: had the Act not been introduced, he would not have entered the business. This respondent had been a landlord in the past but had withdrawn from letting because he believed that the prevailing economic conditions were not conducive to being a landlord. He also made it clear that if a system of rent registration were reintroduced, he would once again withdraw from the business. This previous episode of being a landlord is not an insignificant factor, as only a few of all the respondents had ever been landlords prior to their current letting activities. Thus, with one notable exception, the business landlords had not been motivated by the introduction of the 1988 Act.

Portfolio details

There was a wide variation in the portfolios of the respondents, with *managing agents* usually having responsibility for the largest number of lettings, and *informal sideline landlords* generally having the smallest number of lettings. It was also evident that there were exceptions or unusual cases amongst the different types of respondents.

Managing agents were clearly business oriented with regard to their portfolios. They usually managed a range of properties of varying types and sizes, shared and sole occupancy, and of differing positions in the market. As one managing agent put it: *'Flats, houses, maisonettes, whatever is lettable. If we can let it, we will'*. Some of the managing agents confined their operations to just one area of a city, for example one agent's lettings were almost exclusively on one estate. Others tended to have their business in two or three London Boroughs. At the other extreme, there were two very large businesses with lettings in several different areas of the country.

There was a wide range in the size of the *managing agents* portfolios. One had 30 lettings, whilst another had 12,000 lettings across the country. The two agents with the largest portfolios, were also the two respondents in this category who were also landlords. However, both of them managed far more lettings than the number they themselves owned: one owned about 50 properties but managed 7,000, whilst the other was landlord of 56 lettings but managed 12,000 lettings in total.

Of the landlords in the survey, the *business landlords* usually had the largest portfolios, although again there was variation in this respect. One landlord owned about 100 properties, whilst another had two (one of which was a maisonette which went with a shop premises). The business landlords were the respondents who were most likely to say that some or most of their lettings were bedsits or in houses in multiple occupation. However, none of them were exclusively letting shared accommodation, as they all (with the exception of the landlord with two properties) said that they had lettings in a range of property types.

The *formal sideline landlords* were typically letting two or three properties. The lettings of these landlords were usually in self contained units, either in houses which had been converted into flats, or in whole houses. Once again, however, there were variations to this pattern. One of the landlords owned 20 houses which were let as single lettings, and one resident landlord had converted his home to create 20 bedsits.

There was less variation in portfolios amongst the *informal sideline landlords*. Most of these landlords were letting out one room in their own homes, and were sharing their kitchens, bathrooms and living rooms with their tenants. The exceptions to this pattern were with the two non-resident landlords. One of these had two properties, which had been bought to accommodate his children. The other landlord was letting to a friend who had asked to rent the property upon hearing that the landlord was going to move out and sell it. This landlord was currently living with his parents.

How portfolio was acquired

Portfolio acquisition for the *managing agents* was invariably through advertising in the local press, and to a lesser extent through recommendations from their existing client landlords. In cases where the managing agents were also estate agents, they said that some of their lettings were acquired from people who had come to them to sell, but who were experiencing difficulty in doing so. In these cases the agents had sometimes suggested letting as an interim option for the owner, and occasionally let properties whilst keeping them up for sale.

It was typical for both sub-groups of the *sideline landlords* to have originally bought their property, or one of their properties, with a mortgage as somewhere for themselves or their families to live. This situation was the case for all the *informal landlords*, and for most of the *formal sideline landlords*. Two of the *formal sideline landlords* had inherited the property they were letting, and another had bought his property with the proceeds from the sale of an inherited property. Two of this type of landlord were builders (one was now retired) who had bought run-down properties with a loan, and then renovated them.

Portfolio acquisition for the *business landlords* was generally an on-going process of reinvestment, and in this respect they were markedly different from the sideline landlords. It was common for this type of landlord to have saved up for their first property (or sometimes to have used a business loan), which they then refurbished and subsequently let. Their portfolios expanded as rental income was used to invest in more property, which would often require refurbishing before it was lettable. Thus the business landlords had a career oriented approach to portfolio acquisition. One business landlord now had almost 100 lettings after starting out about eight years previously:

> *We started off by letting rooms because we were short of money. We let rooms in our house, and then we scraped enough together to manage to buy another house and developed that, and went on from there.*

Motivations

Reasons for becoming landlords

The *informal sideline landlords* usually gave one or the other of two main reasons for why they had become landlords. These were either to help their family or friends out; or because they were experiencing financial difficulties and required extra income. A common problem mentioned by these latter landlords was that they needed some extra income to help pay their mortgages, and in this sense rental income was viewed as being very important. One informal landlord said she had started letting because: '...*the house is large and we didn't have enough money to pay the mortgage...That way you could pay a mortgage and be able to pay the bills*'. Rental income was viewed as being less important by those who were helping someone out, although many said that the extra money was useful. The informal sideline landlords generally viewed their lettings as a temporary situation, either saying that they would prefer not to let if they had the choice, or that they may sell if the housing market improves. This type of landlord did not view their lettings in a business-like way, but primarily as their homes.

By comparison, a greater diversity of reasons were given by the *formal sideline landlords* for why they first became involved in letting property. A general theme underlying the reasons given by several of these respondents was that they had become landlords due to force of (invariably financial) circumstances. One respondent even described his landlord origin as an accident. Reasons given by these landlords included the inability to sell the last home when the respondent had moved to another; because the respondent had become unemployed; and letting of the respondent's father's house to pay for his father's care costs. One respondent was continuing to be a landlord against his will because he had returned home from abroad and had been unable to gain repossession of his house. It was common for this group of landlords to view rental income as important, but also to say that they would prefer to sell if house prices picked up.

Investment for the future was another recurring theme given by the *formal sideline landlords* for their reasons for becoming landlords. It was not uncommon for these landlords to view their portfolios as a security for when they retire. As one (retired) landlord put it: '...*the way the government's going on with pensions and one thing or another. ...I've been self-employed all my life, and I wanted a bit of security for when I got old...*'. This group of landlords tended to stress the importance of future rental income, rather than capital gains, for when they were retired.

There were several other reasons given by the *formal sideline landlords* about why they had begun to let, which included that it was initially to help out a friend but had turned out to be a successful way of earning extra income; that it was an alternative source of income when the landlord had taken redundancy to look after his family; and that letting to lodgers was a way of life.

The *business landlords* were most likely to have become landlords because it was viewed as a good way to make a living. One business landlord simply said: '*I look at it as a job*'. In contrast to many of the formal sideline landlords, therefore, the business landlords had made an active choice to become involved in letting. These landlords frequently emphasised the current rental income from their portfolio rather than capital gains in the future. However, two of them did say that capital gains were also important, and that the way they viewed their portfolios depended on the prevailing economic conditions. As one of them put it:

> When you go through the boom years then you're looking at the capital growth, very much so, and then when you hit the recessionary periods you can only look at rentals and you have to orient yourself in that direction...So currently we're looking at rentals, not capital.

Four of the *business landlords* said that they had developed an interest in letting property as a result of other related experiences: one landlord had lived in private rented accommodation and had thought that he could make a better job of it than his landlords had; another had seen his father operating as a landlord and had been keen to enter the business and take over from him. Two other respondents had developed an interest in becoming landlords as a result of their experiences in other property-related occupations (one had been a builder and one had been a surveyor).

Although motivations for becoming a landlord were not applicable to the *managing agents*, two of them had initially been estate agents who had since diversified into lettings. Both of these said that the reason they had diversified was because their income from sales was dropping due to the slump in the owner occupied housing market, and they saw lettings as a linked business. One of them said that they had diversified in order for the business to survive, as they had seen other estate agents in their locality closing down due to lack of trade.

Rate of return on rental income

There has been much debate about the rates of return private landlords can achieve on rental income, and whether they are sufficient to attract new investment into the market. For example, in evidence to the House of Commons Environment Committee in 1981/82, the British Property Federation suggested that a minimum rental yield of nine per cent gross and six per cent net was necessary; and the Small Landlords Association suggested a figure of ten per cent net. However, debates about rates of return on rental income are based on an assumption that private landlords are generally business-minded in their approach to letting, taking into consideration possible alternative investment options.

The *informal sideline landlords* were clearly not business oriented in their approach to letting, and this was a factor which was reflected in their attitudes to rates of return on rental income. Almost all this group of landlords had not given consideration to, or did not know if they were achieving, a return on their capital. This attitude was summed up by one informal landlord:

Well we haven't really ever worked it out. It's been a temporary measure for such a long time really. Just something that would help for a while...it's difficult to assess anyway in one house when the gas and the electricity both went up at the same time... . So we don't actually even know yet what we are making.

One of this group of landlords did say, however, that he aimed to achieve five per cent profit from his rental income, and another that he aimed to make about £30 profit per month. These landlords were the exception, however, and even they, like almost all the other informal sideline landlords, said that they expected their rental income to contribute to their mortgage payments and other costs in their homes. Two of this group of landlords said that the rent was only for a bit of extra income, and wasn't for anything in particular.

As with the informal landlords, the more *formal sideline landlords* generally did not think about a rate of return from rental income. This group of landlords typically said they thought they made a profit from the rent they charged, but that they were not sure exactly how much, and had not considered it in terms of a rate of return. This attitude was summed up by one formal sideline landlord: *'Well I like to put so much away to cover running expenses. At the end of the year if there's nothing major goes wrong, then it's mine and I can enjoy it'.* Others said that they had not considered a rate of return from their rent, and were happy so long as the rent covered their costs. Like the informal sideline landlords, the formal landlords were generally concerned that the rent should cover the mortgages or loans on their properties, and their running costs (maintenance and insurance were frequently specified). One of this type of landlord said that the rent provided an income for him which supplemented his pension.

The *business landlords* were the most likely of all the respondents to have a rate of return from rental income figure in mind. Four of these landlords had at some time made an estimation of a rate of return on rental income: two said they aimed to achieve ten per cent, one worked on the basis of 20 per cent, and one had calculated his return to be six per cent a few years ago. One of the business landlords had not calculated his rate of return, and another stated that he did not have a specific figure in mind as his rents were determined by the market.

Clearly the *business landlords* valued the rent as income, as it was their main occupation and income. However, a few of them also said that the rental income had to cover the costs of their loans or mortgages, as well as their running expenses.

The *managing agents* usually had not given rates of return on rental income any consideration, often saying that any rate of return would be the concern of their landlords, and not themselves. In other instances, the managing agents thought that their landlords did not consider a rate of return, and that they were generally happy so long as the rent covered their mortgages.

Impact of the property slump

The 1991 Census shows that the private rented sector accounted for about 9.4 per cent of all households in England in that year. This proportion is an increase from an all time low of 8.6 per cent in 1989, and a reversal of the continuous trend of decline in the private rented sector since the early years of this century. Evidence from the Labour Force Survey shows that the proportion of households living in the private rented sector has continued to increase since the 1991 Census, to 9.9 per cent in 1993 (Downs *et al*, 1994).

There has been much debate about the reasons for the small reversal in the declining trend of the private sector. For example, some have argued that the increase in size is due to policy initiatives; such as the extension of the Business Expansion Scheme (BES) for lettings on assured tenancies in the private sector, or the introduction of assured shorthold tenancies and the deregulation of rents after the 1988 Housing Act. Others believe that the recent increase in the PRS may be a temporary phenomenon, and that it is largely due to people letting their property as an alternative to selling at the present time, as a result of the slump in the owner occupied housing market. According to this argument, if prices increase, then many of these reluctant landlords will choose to sell, thus withdrawing from the private lettings market.

There were only a few responses elicited from the *informal sideline landlords* about the impact of the property slump. However, two of them who did express a view said that they would prefer to sell but were not able to do so because of the poor state of the owner occupied housing market. Another of this type of landlord said that the property slump had not had any effect on her personally. As the discussion of reasons for becoming landlords showed, however, several of the informal sideline landlords viewed their lettings as a temporary situation, and thought that they may sell up if house prices were to improve.

A commonly expressed view by the *formal sideline landlords* was that they would prefer to sell but could not consider it at the present time because of the depressed prices on the housing market: these landlords said that they would probably sell their property if the market picks up. Contrary to this view, there were two formal landlords who saw the property slump in a more positive fashion. These both relied for their lettings on cheap properties. One of them said that it had been a good time for him to buy, and the other said that if prices started to increase he may have to reconsider his approach to being a landlord.

Business landlords often said that the property slump has had a bearing on their rents. One of these landlords said that the slump had increased the number of properties available for renting, thus giving tenants a greater choice of accommodation and thereby affecting the rents he was able to charge. Two other business landlords felt unable to sell any of their properties, and this had increased the importance of rental income to them in relation to capital gains. One of these landlords also felt that a positive aspect of the slump was that he was able to buy cheap properties, especially repossessions, to contribute to his business. Contrary to this view, however, another business landlord had almost been forced into bankruptcy by the slump in prices: he had lost £150,000 over the last two to three years on some property he was developing. This landlord had withdrawn from letting in the past as a result of other slumps in the property market.

Managing agents, who were arguably the best placed to comment on the property slump due to their contact with a wide range of both landlords and tenants, were all of the opinion that there were more properties available for renting as a result of the down-turn in the market. They thought that there was an increase in people letting because they were having difficulty in selling or because they were trapped in negative equity. Many of these agents also emphasised that as well as the increased supply, there was also an increase in demand from people wanting to rent. This latter group of managing agents generally felt that the increased demand was due to people who had been put off buying, and who as a result were turning to renting instead. One of these agents believed that the property slump would have long-term implications for the private rented sector: '...*the property market for renting will always be there now, because a lot of people have had a bad taste of what the market is, buying properties is not necessarily as good an investment as it was years ago...*'. Another of these agents was also of the opinion that more people were turning to renting because of the increased flexibility offered by this tenure, in comparison with owner occupation, as they were uncertain about their futures.

Summary

The main findings to emerge from this chapter were as follows:

▸	The respondents were not an homogeneous group. Four types of respondent were defined in terms of their basic characteristics, their motivations, and how they viewed their portfolio:

-	*managing agents*
-	*business landlords*
-	*sideline landlords - formally operating*
-	*sideline landlords - informally operating*

▶ None of the *business landlords* were resident landlords. Most of the *formally operating sideline landlords* were not resident landlords, and all except two of the *informally operating sideline landlords* were resident landlords.

▶ Most of the *informally operating sideline landlords* first started to let in 1989 or later. Slightly more of the *formally operating sideline landlords* first started letting in or after 1989 than before then. All the *business landlords* had first started letting before 1989.

▶ The *managing agents* generally had the largest portfolios of all the respondents. Amongst the landlords, the *business landlords* typically owned the largest number of properties; the *formally operating sideline landlords* usually had two or three properties other than their own homes; and the *informally operating sideline landlords* were usually letting one room in their own homes.

▶ *Informal sideline landlords* usually began letting either to help out a friend or member of their own family, or to generate rental income to contribute to their mortgages. The *formally operating sideline landlords* were likely to have begun letting either through force of circumstances (often because they were unable to sell their homes as a result of the slump in the owner occupied housing market), or as an investment for the future. *Business landlords* generally started letting because it was viewed as a good way to make a living.

▶ The *informal sideline landlords* were highly unlikely to have considered rental income in terms of a return on their capital. The more *formally operating sideline landlords* were also unlikely to have calculated a rate of return: some thought they made a profit but were not sure how much, and others were content so long as the rent covered their costs. It was common for the *business landlords* to operate with a rate of return from rental income figure in mind.

▶ The effect of the property slump in the owner occupied market was that many of the *sideline landlords*, particularly those operating in a formal manner, felt unable to sell their properties. Some of the *business landlords* said that the slump had affected the rents they were able to charge because of the increase in property available to rent, and some said that cheap property for sale was available to contribute to their businesses. The *managing agents* said that as a result of the slump there were more people letting who were unable to sell, and more people choosing to rent in preference to buying.

Chapter Three
Feelings About Being a Landlord

Introduction

This chapter considers the respondents' feelings about being a landlord. It looks at how they thought they were viewed as landlords by their tenants, by the Housing Benefit office, by their local authority, and by the general public. The chapter then examines the respondents' views on the positive and negative things about being a landlord. Finally, there is an examination of the respondents' future expectations and intentions.

How they think they are viewed by their tenants

There was a variety of opinion about how the landlords felt they were viewed by their tenants. *Managing agents* generally felt that their tenants thought them to be fair and reasonable. It was common for them to say that they treated their tenants well, and that as a result they had a good reputation. One agent said that their tenants considered them to be the *'good guys'* compared with landlords, as they knew that things would be handled professionally and within the law.

The prevalent attitude amongst the *business landlords* was that some tenants respected them and thought that they were fair, whilst others did not. As one of them put it: *'...some will think I'm horrendous, some will think I'm OK'.* It was not clear why these landlords thought that there were these two opposing views held about them by their tenants, although one business landlord thought that there was a difference between employed tenants and those on Income Support, with the former thinking that he was fair, and the latter treating him with contempt.

The *formal sideline landlords* generally thought that their tenants viewed them as fair landlords. This type of landlord frequently emphasised the friendly nature of their relationship with their tenants. *Informal sideline landlords* placed even more emphasis on this type of relationship with their tenants. Typically, these landlords had not thought about how they were viewed by their tenants, as their relationship was frequently based on a friendship prior to the letting agreement, or one which had developed since then.

Some of the informal landlords felt that their tenants were more than friends, and were now part of their families. When asked how he thought he was viewed as a landlord by his tenant, one *informal sideline landlord* (who was letting to a member of his Jehovahs Witness congregation) said that:

> *...I don't really think of it like that because it's just one room. And the situation at the moment, as I say, it's a brother in our organisation anyway, and he's more or less like one of the family now. We share meals now. Sometimes he comes down and cooks for us as well. So it's more like having a son.*

How they think they are viewed by the Housing Benefit office

Many of the respondents had no opinion about, or did not know, how they were viewed by the Housing Benefit office. Most of those who did express an opinion on the subject felt that the Housing Benefit office did not view them favourably, although there were contrary views to this. One agent felt that the Housing Benefit office viewed them with suspicion, as if they were trying to abuse the system; whilst another felt that they were viewed as reasonable organisations who provided properties too cheaply.

A view expressed by several of the respondents, in relation to them chasing up delays in Housing Benefit claims, was that the Housing Benefit office considered them to be a nuisance. One *business landlord* felt that the Housing Benefit office were so incompetent and slow at handling claims that he had no option other than to constantly pressurise them. As the majority of his tenants were in receipt of Housing Benefit, he viewed this process as a necessary alternative to withdrawing from the business:

> *...I know I am a pain in the arse to the Housing Benefit officers, I know I am. I will remain being a pain in the arse, because the only way I can get any sense out of the Housing Benefit department is by being a pain in the arse. Our local Housing Benefit office currently takes just two telephone enquiries per phone call. After that you've got to put the phone down and phone up again. We do that. We write letters continually; six letters sometimes for the same person. We get no satisfaction out of them. So I am a huge pain in the arse to them, but I'll stay that way, unless I get out of the business which is the other alternative.*

How they think they are viewed by their local authority

Once again, many of the respondents had no opinion about, or did not know, how they were viewed by their local authority. Amongst those who did express an opinion on the issue, a common view was that the local authority did not have a constructive approach to private landlords. One *sideline landlord* thought that they were viewed as an inconvenience, whilst others were of the opinion that they were regarded as unwanted but essential to meet housing needs. As one landlord put it:

> *I would think that landlords in general are viewed by the local authority as a necessary evil, I would think. I would think that probably, if the local authority could afford to maintain and keep sufficient houses for the needs of people in DSS categories, if you like, I would think that's what they would prefer to do.*

Another view, which was commonly mentioned, was that private landlords were seen by the local authority as affluent or profiteering, and sometimes without any concern for the standard of accommodation they provided. One *business landlord* thought that his local authority was not interested in private landlords because landlords were considered to be just after the authority's money.

Contrary to these views, however, there were a few respondents who felt that their local authority viewed them in a more positive way. Those who felt that their local authority had a positive view of landlords often specified a particular department with which they had a good working relationship. One *business landlord* felt that he had a good relationship with the grants department, and another that he had a good relationship with the environmental health department. Another business landlord felt that he was viewed in a different way by the different departments, but that relationships generally were improving from a time when some of the departments had been *'bastards'*. This improvement was largely attributed to the development of a local landlords association, initiated by the respondent, which provided a forum for the discussion of problems between landlords and the local authority.

How they think they are viewed by the general public

There was an overall consensus that the public perceived landlords in an extremely negative way. The terms of reference used in the comments were overwhelmingly of the type 'profiteering for little in return', 'exploiting tenants', and 'sub-standard accommodation'. None of the respondents' comments were in relation to the harassment of tenants, and only one specifically mentioned the eviction of tenants as a public concern.

Several of the respondents emphasised the role of the media in reinforcing a stereotype of landlords as profiteering at the expense of their tenants, and as the providers of sub-standard property. The general view was that media attention exclusively focused on bad landlords without acknowledging the existence of good landlords. Thus, it was clear that the respondents believed that there were bad landlords, but that bad landlords were the exception rather than rule. One *formal sideline landlord* summed up this view:

> *The thing is with the publicity that landlords get, you only ever hear about the bad landlord. If it's on the television it's all blown-up. Nobody ever mentions about the good landlords who care about the property and take an interest in the tenants.*

Related to the respondents' belief in this pejorative view of landlords was the conviction that public opinion was invariably sympathetic towards tenants, irrespective of circumstances. One *business landlord* went so far as to say that the public opinion of landlords was so poor that crimes against them were socially sanctioned:

> *I think landlords are like coppers - all coppers are bastards and all landlords are bastards. I think that's the general impression one gets, isn't it. It's perfectly socially acceptable to steal from the landlord - I would say that's a quite acceptable thing: 'Oh, I ran off owing so much money', 'Oh, great, wow'.*

Underpinning these views about how they think the public perceived them, was the sense of injustice at the popular stereotypes. Two general views were related to this opinion: that landlords were simply trying to do a difficult job; and that there was such a variety of different types of landlords that the Rachman image was widely unrepresentative. As one *informal landlord* put it:

> *...most people don't think of people like me, just renting out one room, do they? They think about these multi-millionaires who have made their money by exploiting people who need rented accommodation. They just think of the ones that have a big profile like Rachman and that sort of thing.*

Positive things about being a landlord

Reflecting the fact that being a landlord was their full-time occupation, the *business landlords* most commonly thought that a positive aspect to being a landlord was that it provided them with a living. This type of landlord also felt that they were providing a service to meet a need. Other positive things mentioned included that some tenants gave their landlord presents to show their gratitude, and that the landlord's portfolio was something which could be handed down to his family. Two business landlords said that a positive thing about their occupation was that they enjoyed it. As one of them put it:

> *I get a hell of a kick from getting an old derelict three story property, stripping it down to bare walls and little else, and walking away from it*

six months later having converted it into a beautiful three or four flatted house. Now I get a buzz out of that. I also get a buzz out of knowing that I'm giving decent accommodation to people.

Few of the *managing agents* felt able to speak on their landlords' behalf. Those who did, however, thought that a benefit was that their landlords' properties were not left empty, and that the landlord had rental income with which to pay their mortgages.

Rental income and the fact that they were providing a service, were two of the positive things mentioned by the *formal sideline landlords*. Another positive aspect given by this type of landlord was that their property was an investment for future rental income. One landlord said that the positive thing was that the property was a security for his family in the event of anything happening to him.

Almost all the *informal sideline landlords* who expressed an opinion said that the positive thing about being a landlord was the company of having a lodger, or the friendship they had with them. Of a student lodger who had recently had to leave, one such landlord said:

> *...we used to watch television together some nights for company, and we'd take the dog out for a walk. We got on fantastic. We gave a little party before she went. We all had tears. She didn't want to go, but she failed so she had to go.*

Two of the informally operating landlords said that a positive thing was that they felt more secure with someone else living with them, rather than being on their own.

Negative things about being a landlord

A range of negative aspects were specified by the *business landlords*. One said that there was so much to learn that he had made expensive mistakes along the way. This respondent also stressed the labour-intensive nature of being a landlord as a problem - he performed all the management himself as well as carried out minor repairs and redecorations. Other business landlords emphasised the problems involved in dealing with official departments: one landlord mentioned the courts, which he felt favoured tenants; and another mentioned the delays and red tape he had experienced with Housing Benefit.

One business landlord pointed to the stress involved (as did some of the other types of landlords), from what he saw as constant aggravation from all sides:

> *...in my wallet there are two aspirins. That's for my heart attack, and I'm not kidding. The stress is incredible, because at any one time I can get*

> *descended upon by any one of ten inspectors. ... If my tenants rip out the*
> *fire alarm system I am responsible. If my tenants leave furniture in the*
> *passageway and somebody gets killed, I'm responsible. My tenants*
> *regularly - the worst ones - threaten to kill me, do this and do that.*
> *...Dealing with local authority bureaucracy, red tape, that drives me to*
> *distraction, and virtual bankruptcy. ...I've continually got a headache,*
> *and I'm continually being kicked from pillar to post.*

This particular landlord was in the throes of taking his local authority to court, because he felt they were breaking the law by not giving grants for houses in multiple occupation, which he thought should be paid mandatorily. He said that the stress was such that he was seriously considering closing his business.

Once again, few of the *managing agents* were able to comment, although two who did said that the major problem was the risk of getting bad tenants. These agents felt that it was difficult to know what a tenant would be like at the outset, and that landlords could unwittingly let to someone who wrecks their property or who refuses to leave at the end of the agreement. One of these agents thought that the negative problem of the risk involved so outweighed any positive aspects to letting, that his initial advice to his landlords was: *'If you don't have to let your house, don't do it, because it is an unknown quantity'*. Many of this agent's landlords were letting their homes temporarily, possibly expecting to live in them again. This he saw as a the major motivation for his advice, as he believed that people typically were emotionally attached to their homes, and that having bad tenants could cause a great deal of anguish.

The most commonly mentioned negative things about being a landlord by the *formal sideline landlords* were to do with the trouble involved. Some simply said that being a landlord was troublesome, whilst others were resentful that they were always on call even for trivial matters. Another of these landlords mentioned the time and money involved in preparing the letting for a new tenant, and others pointed to the stress involved. The other negative things mentioned by this type of landlord were mostly to do with having bad tenants, that is, tenants who were noisy or persistently in rent arrears.

The negative things mentioned by the *informal sideline landlords* were generally about sharing their homes with someone else. These included problems with sharing facilities (such as a queue for the bathroom), that the friendship may become strained or they may not get on with their lodger, and that the tenant may be a security risk (leaving doors and windows unlocked).

Future intentions

In addition to the Government's concern of recent years to stimulate the private rented sector, by introducing several supply-side measures (the extension of the business expansion scheme for assured lettings; the 1988 Housing Act, which introduced assured shorthold tenancies and deregulated new rents; and the introduction of the accelerated possession procedure in November 1993), there is a new emphasis on using the private rented sector to house statutory homeless households (DoE, 1994).

It is therefore clear that the sustainability, if not the expansion, of the private rented sector is seen by many to be either desirable or necessary. As discussed in chapter two, however, many of the respondents in this survey were reluctant to be involved in letting, many of them viewing it as a temporary solution to their current financial difficulties. Therefore, it is important to know what landlords intend to do in the future and why; and also to what extent, if any, intentions coincided with desires.

Generally, there was a difference between the *business landlords* and *managing agents* on the one hand, and the two types of *sideline landlords* on the other. This difference was one relating to the certainty of future intentions: business landlords and agents were usually quite clear about what they intended to do over the next few years, whilst the sideline landlords were often far less sure. In many respects, the future actions of the *sideline landlords* were contingent upon external factors over which they often had little or no control. In relation to this situation, many of the sideline landlords' future expectations diverged from what they would actually have preferred to do.

There were two basic strategies for the future amongst the *business landlords*: either a continuation of their on-going processes of portfolio expansion, or to maintain their portfolio at or about its current size. In some respects, this latter group could be described as consolidating their positions as landlords. None of the business landlords expected to pursue a process of systematic disinvestment, although one of the landlords, who was expecting to maintain his portfolio as it stood, said that he intended to sell off two properties which he had bought at a very low price.

The typical expectation of the *managing agents* was that the number of properties they managed would continue to increase, as it had done over the past few years. Two of the agents said that the lettings portfolios would increase because of the recent trend towards renting in preference to owner occupation. However, one agent said that he would not increase his lettings portfolio, but that this was because he was so busy handling the properties he already managed. Another agent was hoping to expand his portfolio by trying to attract business from landlords who were managing their own properties, but who were having difficulties doing so. As with the business landlords, none of the agents intended or expected the number of lettings they managed to decrease.

As noted above, there was often a divergence between the future expectations and the desires of the *sideline landlords*. Invariably, this situation was the result of them being unsure about what may happen in the near future. Many of these landlords would have preferred to sell their properties, but as they did not think that they would get a good price on the owner occupier market, were expecting to continue letting for the time being. One *informal landlord* was letting out a room in her house while she was a student, and would continue to do so until she was able to find a job; a *formal sideline landlord* thought that he would probably continue to let provided his building society was agreeable.

Some of both types of *sideline landlords* thought that there would be no change to their letting situations in the forseeable future, but two *informal sideline landlords* said that when their present lodgers (who were friends) had left they would not let again. Four of the *formally operating sideline landlords* said that they expected or hoped to increase the size of their portfolios. One of these was a builder who required an office from which to run his business, and wanted to obtain premises which included a flat; and one was a retired builder who was talking with his son about the possibility of buying some land to build on.

The other two *formal sideline landlords* who were hoping to expand could be described as embryonic business landlords. One of these landlords thought that he would continue buying properties and doing them up, but would stop this process before it became necessary to take someone on to help run the business, as that is when they thought he would start to lose out financially. The other landlord had a clear view of the future, and intended to build up the business until it provided an income:

> *...we can see how much people have progressed in a relatively short amount of time, and have become quite wealthy through it. So we can see a goal at the end of it, and that's what we would like to aim at. ...my husband will be forty in seven years time, and he'd like to be at a stage where he doesn't have to go to work every day at that stage. So that's what we are aiming at. We will hopefully get this second house, and possibly a third one by that time.*

Summary

The main findings to emerge from this chapter were as follows:

▶   *Managing agents* thought that they were viewed positively by their tenants, and often as the 'good guys' compared with landlords. *Business landlords* said that some of their tenants would view them positively and some negatively. *Sideline landlords* frequently emphasised the friendly nature of the relationships with their tenants, and this was particularly the case for those operating informally.

▶ Many respondents were not sure how they were viewed by their Housing Benefit office. However, many thought that their Housing Benefit office viewed them unfavourably or with suspicion. Some landlords said that they had a bad relationship with their Housing Benefit office because they considered them to be slow and incompetent at processing claims.

▶ Many respondents were also unsure how their local authority regarded them. Several thought that their local authority did not have a constructive approach to private landlords, and some thought that they were viewed as a necessary evil to meeting housing needs.

▶ All the respondents thought that the general public had very negative views of private landlords. This situation was often thought to be perpetuated by the media's attention to bad landlords without acknowledging the existence of good landlords.

▶ *Business landlords* were frequently of the opinion that the positive thing about being a landlord was that it provided them with an income. The *formal sideline landlords* commonly mentioned rental income, and also that it was an investment for the future. The *informal sideline landlords* said the positive thing about being a landlord was the company and friendship of having a lodger.

▶ Negative things mentioned by the *business landlords* included the problems they had experienced with the courts and the administration of Housing Benefit. The high level of stress involved was also considered a negative aspect to being a landlord. The *formal sideline landlords* frequently mentioned the trouble involved, and the *informal sideline landlords* mentioned problems with sharing facilities and strains on the friendships with their lodgers.

▶ The *managing agents* and *business landlords* were generally confident that in the future they would either maintain their portfolios at the same size or expand. *Sideline landlords* were generally less sure about the future, some saying that they were unlikely to change their number of lettings in the forseeable future, and others saying that they may sell if prices in the owner occupied market improved.

Chapter Four
Managing the Property

Introduction

This chapter considers the respondents' experiences of managing their property. It looks firstly at the landlords' use and experiences of managing agents. Secondly, the chapter looks at how tenants were found, and the respondents' attitudes to rent in advance and deposits. Next there is a consideration of rent guarantees, including views on direct payments of Housing Benefit as a rent guarantee. The next part of the chapter looks at the types of tenancy agreements used, and the respondents' views on them. Finally, the chapter examines experiences of rent arrears and evictions through the courts.

Use of manging agents

Only a few of the landlords in the survey used, or had ever used, an agent. None of the *informal sideline landlords* or the *business landlords* (except one who very occasionally used an agent to find tenants) were making use of agents: both types were performing the management of their letting(s) completely by themselves.

On the other hand, however, some (but not all) of the *formal sideline landlords* were using agents, a factor which may be related to their relative distance from their properties. With one exception, a respondent who was retired, the formal sideline landlords were in full-time employment; nearly all of them were non-resident landlords; and they were future oriented in their motivations, either anticipating selling when property prices increase, or viewing their lettings as an investment for when they retired. This position contrasts with the *business landlords* and the *informal landlords*, who were closely involved with their lettings (either because it was their occupation or because the tenants lived in their homes), and whose motivations were oriented towards accruing rental income for the present.

Thus, *formal sideline landlords* tended to have a comparatively 'arms-length' approach to letting, and tended to use managing agents to organise agreements and find tenants. This last function in particular landlords preferred to leave to agents. As one landlord put it: *'There is nothing worse than meeting people, or the phone keeps ringing with people after flats. We have tried, and it's a nuisance'.* Even so, however, these landlords were not wholly distant from their tenants, as they were frequently the first port of call for repairs, and with one exception they collected the rent themselves.

The views on using managing agents, by those who had used them, were mixed. Generally, landlords said that they had a good relationship with their agent, and were very happy with the services they received. However, some felt that the quality of the services they received varied from one agent to another. Dissatisfaction with agents was usually expressed in terms of a high cost for little in return, that is, these landlords were involved with their properties more than they would have preferred. One *formal sideline landlord* who had used an agent in the past did not expect to use one again: *'No. It's not worth it. Yes if somebody was taking all the responsibility, yes, I would be willing to give 10 per cent, even more. But they don't'.*

Finding tenants

A range of methods were used by the respondents for finding tenants, and most said that finding tenants was easy. The *managing agents* were well organised in their approach to finding tenants, their main approach usually being the placing of regular advertisements in local newspapers. Other methods were used to supplement the advertisements, such as notices in local shops, having tenants referred to them from local authority housing agency centres, and advertising on university accommodation lists.

Reflecting the views expressed by many of the *managing agents* that there had been an increase in the number of people wanting to rent (see chapter two), several operated waiting lists. Commenting on the ease with which tenants were found, one agency said of their waiting list ('register') that: *'...as soon as properties are in, they're gone. And sometimes we don't even get to open the register before someone walks in the door'.* An opinion expressed by several agents, however, was that demand from people wanting to rent was subject to seasonal fluctuations. Filling vacancies during the summer months was generally thought to be easier than during other parts of the year, at which times more effort had to be devoted to finding tenants. Another agency felt that finding tenants was a completely unpredictable process, as it depended on the price and location of the property, and where it was advertised.

One agent found it difficult to find tenants, the reason being that its client landlords were stipulating with increasing regularity that they would only let to people who were not on Housing Benefit. The agent generally found it much more difficult to find tenants who were not on Housing Benefit than those who were. The agency had experienced many difficulties with Housing Benefit tenants due to delays in the processing of claims; tenants not paying their rent although they were receiving Housing Benefit; the local authority reclaiming overpayments of Housing Benefit after periods of up to one year; and the courts being biased against managing agencies and landlords. These collective problems had influenced landlords' letting strategies: *'So here you have a situation that 90 per cent of people who can afford it, they don't rent now to people who are unemployed'*. Over a period of two years, the agency had gone from letting almost exclusively to Housing Benefit tenants, to currently having only two (from a total of about 100 lettings).

The landlords in the survey tended to be slightly more informal than the managing agents in the ways in which they found their tenants, although some did place advertisements in the local press. *Business landlords* in particular used the local press, but also commonly said that they found tenants by word of mouth, or through a mixture of the two methods. Other methods used included advertisements in local shops, and recommendations from their tenants. Business landlords generally said that it was easy for them to find tenants. Only one of them was experiencing difficulty finding tenants, and this was due to the local university increasing accommodation for its students. This situation had created a void in the local market, leading to increased competition from other landlords for a reduced tenant population.

As noted above, the *formal sideline landlords* often used letting agents to find their tenants for them. Other landlords of this type relied upon word of mouth, recommendations, or advertisements in local shops. One formal sideline landlord found many of her tenants through referrals from local advice agencies. Typically, this type of landlord found tenants easily. It was emphasised by one, however, that finding people in work (his preferred choice) was difficult compared with finding tenants in receipt of Housing Benefit.

The *informal sideline landlords* generally found their tenants in a relatively casual manner. Several relied on word of mouth, and several had not 'found' tenants at all, but were simply helping someone out. None of this type of landlord had advertised for tenants in the local press, some commenting that it was too expensive to do so. Two informal landlords had found their tenants by putting notices in local shops, one by responding to an advertisement made by a local college requiring accommodation for its students, and another had put a notice in a local arts centre frequented by students. One landlord had found his tenant through his Jehovah's Witness congregation. All these landlords said they had found their tenants easily.

Deposits and rent in advance

Landlords generally required a deposit and rent in advance. Most typically, this took the form of a month's rent as deposit with a further month required as rent in advance. Business landlords and agents tended to be more stringent than other types of landlord in this matter although not exclusively so. One agent, for example, did not expect a deposit and asked for only one week's rent in advance. The requirements of sideline landlords were more varied. Many of the latter asked for a deposit and rent in advance. However, landlords who let on a more informal basis tended to ask for neither.

Deposits and rent in advance were viewed by landlords as important forms of security. Nevertheless, many found that in practice they had to modify their requirements in relation to the financial circumstances of incoming tenants. As in previous research (Thomas and Hedges, 1986) a number of landlords stated that they often found that it was difficult to obtain a deposit or rent in advance from tenants on Housing Benefit.

The attitudes of landlords to this issue were varied. Many suggested that although they would have liked the security of a full deposit and rent in advance, they recognised the limited financial means of many tenants and were prepared to be flexible and negotiate. Often a reduced amount of money was accepted as a deposit, or tenants were expected to make up the amount at a later date.

> Obviously you do get the odd problem with deposits because we also cater for people on DSS, who can't always afford the equivalent of a month's rent for the deposit. So we try to negotiate on that, with the landlord as well, because we know that most of them tend to be tight in that sector, so we do our best.

The willingness of respondents to negotiate depended to a certain extent on judgements of a tenant's character. If a tenant was perceived as a 'good risk', then some landlords seemed more likely to accept a reduced deposit or smaller amount of rent in advance.

However, a few landlords stated that they would not accept tenants who were unemployed or on Housing Benefit unless they could provide a full deposit. Such landlords tended to be more flexible with tenants in employment, who were perhaps perceived as a better 'risk'. In these cases, landlords said they were prepared to accept reduced amounts, staggered payments or rent in advance only.

There was a general feeling among those landlords who required a deposit and rent in advance that it was important for tenants to provide some form of payment at the outset of a tenancy, even if it could only be a reduced amount. One business landlord felt that:

There are always certain people who have not got the deposit, but it is something we always insist on. We wouldn't let anyone move in without a deposit. We might be a little bit lenient on the month's rent in advance depending on if he was working or not. If he wasn't working I might be a little bit more lenient on that, which I have been in the past.

A couple of landlords amplified this point and felt it was essential for tenants to have some form of financial stake in the property, to encourage them to look after it and keep it in reasonable condition.

Landlords' attitudes as to the actual usefulness of deposits were mixed. For a number of landlords deposits provided a cushion against rent arrears. However this meant that when a tenant eventually left, there was no deposit to cover any damage caused. Landlords were also critical of tenants using the deposit as the last month's rent before moving out as this left them with no security at the end of the tenancy. Some landlords commented that whilst the amount they could reasonably expect was sufficient in most cases to cover any damage caused, it was entirely inadequate to cover the cost of any serious damage sustained to a property. Many respondents were particularly fearful of instances where tenants were intent on causing wilful damage, or stealing fixtures and fittings, although these were thought to be rare.

One agent commented that the issue of returning deposits at the end of tenancies was often a cause of dispute between landlords and tenants. This mainly revolved around the interpretation of reasonable wear and tear, and he felt that a number of landlords often tried to withhold a deposit on unreasonable grounds. On the other hand, one landlord stated that he had been intimidated into handing over the deposit at the end of a tenancy, as the tenants had threatened to smash all the windows in the property unless the deposit was returned in full.

Rent guarantees

Kemp and McLaverty (1995) highlight the difficulty that many prospective tenants experience in meeting access costs to privately rented accommodation. Interest has been growing in schemes which offer rent or deposit guarantees to landlords, which are seen as a cost effective method by which various agencies including local authorities can become involved in enabling access to the private rented sector. Attention has particularly focused on the use of such schemes to help house the homeless within the private rented sector (Jenn, 1994). This section of the report explores landlord attitudes to rent guarantees.

Very few landlords had direct experience of rent guarantees and many were not aware of their existence or knew what they might involve. Business landlords and agents were more likely than other types of landlord to have had contact with schemes or to be aware of them.

Generally landlords were in principle quite receptive to the idea of accepting a guarantee. Sideline landlords in particular seemed amenable to the idea, although a number did have reservations.

There was a view that whilst the idea of a rent guarantee itself was attractive, landlords were wary of the type of tenant they would accept. Some landlords would not be prepared to accept a guarantee for this reason. Other respondents felt that they would certainly consider accepting a guarantee, but only if they had extreme difficulty in finding a tenant for a property.

Business landlords and agents who were aware of rent guarantee schemes expressed a number of reservations. Some respondents stated that they were concerned about the increased potential for damage as a result of accepting a 'riskier' tenant. There was the suggestion that firm assurances about compensation for damage to property as part of a guarantee would be more important to them than the guarantee of rent itself.

Other landlords expressed interest in the idea, but felt that they would want the exact terms and conditions of a scheme to be clearly laid out prior to becoming involved. There was a feeling that, as landlords, they would want to be able to see exactly what they would be committing themselves to. As a managing agent put it:

> *We want more and more written guarantees about these things before considering them in the future.*

Blake (1994) highlights the sort of misunderstandings that can arise between landlords' expectations of a rent guarantee scheme and what it will actually deliver. For example, a particular area of concern surrounds the situation where a rent guarantee is offered to a landlord but subsequently a shortfall arises between the rent expected and the amount covered by Housing Benefit as a result of a restriction in eligible rent. One landlord was very wary of accepting a rent guarantee without clear, written conditions for this very reason. The landlord had accepted a rent guarantee in the past and thought a rent had been agreed, only to find that subsequently Housing Benefit would cover only a proportion of the rent.

It has been suggested that the success of rent guarantee schemes could be undermined by delays in Housing Benefit payments (Randall and Brown, 1994). Chapter five highlights the difficulty many landlords experience with respect to the time it takes to process

Housing Benefit claims. In recognition of this issue, a number of rent guarantee schemes offer fast track processing of Housing Benefit claims to provide a further incentive to landlords. This problem was identified by a number of landlords who said that they would be more concerned about receiving Housing Benefit on time than they would about having the security of a guarantee.

A couple of landlords suggested that if Housing Benefit was administered correctly and on time, then personally they would be happy with this and would not necessarily seek an additional guarantee. One business landlord considered that he would be prepared to accept a guarantee, but felt that:

> *I mean the homeless, I'm willing to help them, but that's if...I mean the council say 'We'll do this, we'll do that...' but if they were to pay landlords on time, I guarantee a lot of landlords would take the homeless anyway, because I would.*

Receiving Housing Benefit direct as a form of guarantee

Chapter five highlights the importance that many landlords place upon having Housing Benefit paid direct to them. Many rent guarantee schemes explicitly recognise this fact and require Housing Benefit to be paid direct to the landlord as part of the guarantee (Jenn, 1994; Miller, 1994). This section of the chapter explores how far landlords view Housing Benefit paid direct as a guarantee.

Most respondents generally viewed Housing Benefit direct as a form of guarantee. Many emphasised that it gave them a degree of security in that they could be sure of receiving the rent: *'It gives you peace of mind. It's there and you can budget'*. Part of the perception of Housing Benefit direct as a guarantee stemmed from an enhanced feeling of control over the money and the ability to monitor rent payments more closely. A letting agent felt that *'We know for a fact that we will receive it, and it's monitored a lot better as well. We know what's happening there'*. One landlord considered that payments of Housing Benefit direct gave an incentive to landlords who might otherwise be very wary of accepting tenants on Housing Benefit.

However, a number of other landlords explained why they did not see Housing Benefit direct as a guarantee. Some stressed two key elements of the current system which in their view worked against the interests of landlords. One was that the system of receiving Housing Benefit direct made landlords responsible for overpayments, and secondly that a tenant could still legally have the payments redirected back to themselves. Other landlords did not view Housing Benefit direct in terms of a guarantee as such, but just as a simplified method of receiving the rent.

Tenancy agreements

All business landlords and managing agents had some form of written agreement for their assured, assured shorthold or regulated tenancies. Formal sideline landlords tended to use assured shorthold agreements or assured tenancies although these latter could be written or verbal. Most sideline landlords that let informally had what they described as a verbal agreement and this tended to be conducted on a very casual basis.

The most popular type of agreement was the assured shorthold tenancy, particularly among business landlords and managing agents. One agent commented that this was the only form of agreement that banks and building societies would allow their clients with mortgages on properties to use.

The extent of knowledge about the legislation surrounding tenancy agreements varied considerably between landlords. Business landlords and agents tended to have precise, in depth knowledge of the tenancy agreements they used, although this was by no means universal. A couple of managing agents had portfolios which consisted mainly of regulated tenancies, and whilst the managing agents involved had a working knowledge of these types of agreement, they were less clear about the nature of agreements created in the 1988 Housing Act. One managing agent thought that if an assured shorthold tenancy was renewed too often, then it became an assured tenancy. Another managing agent had recently discovered that he had made an error with his tenancy agreements and the assured shorthold tenancies he thought he had arranged were in fact all assured tenancies.

Most formal sideline landlords said they used assured shorthold agreements. A number of landlords relied upon a letting agent or a solicitor to arrange the details of agreements. However, not all of the landlords who relied on agents were clear about to the type of tenancy they were committed to. Another landlord had recycled an agreement from an earlier tenancy which had been arranged through an agent, but freely admitted that he was not really aware of its contents.

Whilst most sideline landlords letting informally had a verbal agreement with their tenants a number did have a written agreement. One landlord had introduced the word 'shorthold' into his agreement after 1988 but said that he did not know if this made a difference. In another instance the landlord and tenant had made a verbal agreement at the outset of a tenancy, and later changed this to a written agreement to satisfy some third party such as the Housing Benefit office.

Another landlord had deliberately not signed a written agreement because she was worried about committing herself to a tenancy for longer than she wished. she did not seem aware of her rights as a resident landlord in terms of issuing a notice to quit.

In general the use of assured shorthold tenancies was viewed quite positively by landlords and agents. There was a general feeling that the introduction of this type of agreement had been a significant improvement for landlords. One agent stressed that assured shorthold tenancies gave more security to landlords and were preferable to assured tenancies. A number of agents suggested that it was beneficial for both tenants and landlords as both parties had a clearer idea of their legal position and generally knew where they stood in terms of a tenancy. One business landlord felt that assured shorthold tenancies were very useful as kind of probationary tenancy. He felt that it was important to have a new tenant on a six month agreement before committing himself to a longer tenancy:

> It's really very good because you don't know anybody until you try them out really. With a six months...basically if someone new did move in, it's got to be six months. With six months you can tell what they are like, and if you are not happy you can give them their notice, and therefore terminate the contract.

Crook *et al* (1995) found that whilst there was general satisfaction amongst landlords with Assured Shorthold tenancies, the length of time that it took to gain repossession of properties was still an issue. This seemed to be borne out by the attitude of a number of landlords and agents who felt that there was still room for improvement in this area. One business landlord felt that *'The forms themselves are probably okay. It's the courts that go with them, isn't it'*. A number of landlords and agents highlighted the difficulty of maintaining a balance between the needs of the landlord and the rights of the tenant. There was a view that, whilst it was important to ensure that tenants in general retained adequate security, it should be made easier to gain possession in cases where it could be shown that a tenant had seriously defaulted on an agreement.

Rent arrears

A variety of comments were made about rent arrears. First, there were 11 *landlords* who simply had not experienced any rental arrears, and therefore the issue was not of relevance to them personally. These landlords were all *sideline landlords*, four of whom were formally operating, and seven were informally operating landlords. Amongst those who had experienced arrears, however, there were several general themes to the ways in which they usually responded to, or felt about, the problem. The most common themes were that the problem of arrears could be tackled in the first instance by negotiating with the tenant and trying to come to some arrangement; that their experience of arrears was related to Housing Benefit, either in its administration or because of the tenants themselves; and that they reluctantly accepted that arrears were a hazard associated with letting, which sometimes involved them writing off the debts.

Most frequently, the managing agents said that if a tenant got into arrears they would negotiate with them and try to come to an agreement whereby the debt could be settled. It was generally felt that tenants were not usually bad payers, but that some had financial difficulties from time to time, which could be accommodated with negotiation. The agents felt that it was proper for them to take a reasonable line with tenants who were in arrears, a view which was summed up by one who said that: *'Well we all get into arrears over something. We all have a credit card, we all have a cheque that bounces, we all have bills that we have to ask people to wait for; that happens in life'.*

The agents' primary concern regarding arrears was that they should be informed by the tenant in question as soon as a problem arose; in that way they felt more willing and able to sort out a satisfactory solution for both the tenant and the landlord. It was generally felt that problems with arrears could be tackled if they were not allowed to get out of hand. Once the problem was allowed to become serious, agents felt that as the last resort there was little they could do other than begin eviction proceedings:

> *...the worst scenario is when the rent stops and they won't say why. You can't get hold of them, and it just piles up and up. If someone comes in and says 'I'm in trouble at the moment. I'm going to be a bit late paying my rent for the next couple of months, can you do something?' Great, I can judge it, I can work on it, I know what's happening. But if they don't pay and they don't talk to me, I can only get the big stick out. And then it's a case of going to court and getting possession...*

Negotiating with tenants in arrears and coming to an arrangement to sort out the arrears was the usual approach taken by two of the business landlords. Again, it was also emphasised that serious arrears were more difficult to handle, and that evictions may become necessary. A further two of the business landlords said that they had a lot of arrears, but that these were usually due to Housing Benefit delays. One of these landlords said that he put as much pressure on tenants in arrears as he legally was able to do, and would evict if the situation became too bad. A further two business landlords reluctantly accepted arrears as a hazard of their line of work, saying that they sometimes had to write them off. One of these landlords said that he would take repossession action, whilst the other avoided legal proceedings because of the high costs resulting from the length of time the action took.

The formal sideline landlords most commonly said that rent arrears were the result of having tenants in receipt of Housing Benefit (Housing Benefit will be dealt with in more detail in chapters five and six). Delays in the processing of Housing Benefit claims were the cause of the problem for some of these landlords. These delays were often accepted as standard, with the landlords saying that they had little option but to wait for the rent to come through. However, two of the landlords said that they now avoided taking

Housing Benefit tenants because of the problems they have had in the past with processing delays. Some of the landlords had experienced problems with arrears when their Housing Benefit tenants had redirected the payments from the landlords to themselves, and then not paid the rent.

Most of the informal sideline landlords did not have any experience of rent arrears. Those who did, however, said that the problem tended to be the result of delays in Housing Benefit administration rather than wilfulness: '...*sometimes they got very behind with the rent, but never deliberately as it were, either because the housing benefit hadn't come through, or whatever'*. This landlord said that he would never evict someone because of arrears due to Housing Benefit delays. Another informal sideline landlord, however, could not get his tenant to pay the rent even though he was receiving Housing Benefit. In this instance the landlord eventually had to evict the tenant.

Evictions and dealing with the courts

Eviction through the courts was generally the respondents' last recourse when they had tenants who were in serious arrears. Indeed, several respondents said that they would avoid taking a tenant to court because of the perceived problems associated with the procedure. Most commonly, it was felt that arrears and other tenant problems could be resolved by negotiation and reaching some sort of agreement. It was also clear that it was often unnecessary to resort to legal proceedings in order to gain possession, as tenants would often leave when asked to do so.

However, about half the respondents had at some time dealt with evictions through the courts, and all of them gave negative rather than positive accounts of their experiences. Three problems were repeatedly mentioned: that the evictions procedure was very costly; that the process was too long and drawn-out; and that the courts system was biased in the tenants' favour.

Only two of the formally operating sideline landlords and none of the informal sideline landlords had ever evicted through the courts. Most of the managing agents and the business landlords had some experience of pursuing evictions through the courts, both mentioning similar types of problems. Almost all these respondents said that the process took far too long, and was a problem which frequently exacerbated the extent of rent arrears. Several of the respondents felt that there should be a faster procedure for evicting problem tenants; this was in spite of the accelerated possession procedure, of which they clearly were not aware. A specific difficulty mentioned in connection with the lengthy eviction process was that it took about two months to get a date for a court hearing, and there was the fear that the tenant could cause further delays by saying they were unavailable to attend. One agent felt that the delays were particularly unfair when tenants were in arrears and the landlords were relying on the rent to pay their mortgages. Another agent was reluctant to use the courts, but felt that it was sometimes unavoidable in order to preserve his business reputation.

A second major theme to the criticisms of the courts system was the high legal expenses incurred. Often this problem was related to the length of time it could take to complete the whole procedure, but was also connected to the accumulating arrears in the meantime. One business landlord reported that a single eviction had cost him about £8,000.

The third commonly mentioned difficulty with evictions was the feeling that the courts acted more favourably towards the tenants. It was clear that some of the respondents felt that the courts discriminated against landlords, and that they needed more legal protection against problem tenants, particularly with respect to tenants in serious arrears:

> But the law is weak, though, really. For bad payers, it's not strong enough, is it? To think they've got to be three months in arrears, seems stupid. You know you're not going to get the money. ...I've never, ever had anyone pay back the money. It always ends up with them legging it.

Summary

The main findings to emerge from this chapter were as follows:

▸   Business landlords and informally operating sideline landlords were managing their lettings entirely by themselves. Some of the formally operating sideline landlords were using lettings agents, most commonly to find tenants and organise the letting agreements.

▸   A range of methods were used to find tenants. Managing agents and business landlords commonly advertised in the local press, and sideline landlords tended to rely more on recommendations and word of mouth. Nearly all the respondents said they found tenants easily.

▸   Landlords generally required some form of deposit and rent in advance. Many viewed these as an important form of security. However, many respondents said that they recognised the limited financial means of incoming tenants and often were prepared to negotiate on the amount of money that they were prepared to accept.

▸   Many landlords felt that they would be amenable to the idea of accepting a rent guarantee. A number of respondents felt that they would want precise details as to what a guarantee would cover and how such a scheme might work in practice, especially in relation to Housing Benefit.

- Housing Benefit sent direct to landlords was viewed by many respondents as a form of guaranteed payment of rent. But a few respondents felt that the attraction of this element of the Housing Benefit system was attenuated by the ability of tenants to have payment redirected back to themselves, occasionally resulting in loss of rental income.

- The most popular type of agreement amongst landlords who knew what type of agreement they were using was the assured shorthold tenancy.

- Although most business landlords and agents had an in depth knowledge of the type of agreement they were using, it was clear that many sideline landlords had limited knowledge of the legislation surrounding tenancy agreements.

- There were three themes to the views on rent arrears: that the arrears could be tackled by negotiating with tenants and arriving at a solution; that the problem was related to Housing Benefit, either through delays or because of the tenants themselves; and that arrears were a hazard associated with letting, which may involve them being written off.

- Very few of the sideline landlords had evicted any tenants through the courts, but most of the letting agents and business landlords had. Evictions through the courts were seen as the last resort when tenants were in serious arrears. The eviction process was thought to take too long, was considered too expensive, and was seen to favour the tenants.

Chapter Five
Letting Strategies

Introduction

This chapter focuses upon landlords' letting strategies. It examines their letting preferences, including their attitudes towards letting to people on Housing Benefit. It looks at what landlords would see as the 'ideal tenant' and how they select tenants in practice. It also explores landlords' views on the possible introduction of rent ceilings and pre-tenancy determinations. Finally, it examines whether landlords would consider letting to homeless households.

Tenant Preferences

Many landlords had firm ideas about the types of people that they wanted as tenants. To a certain extent, the stated preferences of landlords were affected by the type and size of accommodation that was being let. Nevertheless, many respondents felt that they favoured certain types of people in preference to others. In contrast, a number of landlords stated that they did not have a preference for any particular types of tenant.

Many landlords stated that they did not want to let to young single people. This is significant because these form the largest demand group for new lettings (Kemp, 1990). An informal sideline landlord felt that,

> *Well, I just wouldn't want a young lad, or a young girl that's going to bring all her friends back and have parties and things like that, and I can't do a thing about it.*

Attitudes to letting accommodation to students were mixed. Some landlords commented that they would not like to let to students partly because of the perceived difficulties that this group would cause but also because it was felt that students tended to be very transient and required very short stays in accommodation. However it was this latter feature which was important to one resident landlord as she was concerned about regaining possession. Another informal sideline landlord preferred to let to students because she felt that they were 'safe', and would not cause trouble.

Attitudes of landlords to other types of tenant were also mixed. Many landlords stated that they would not consider families. In part, this was a function of the suitability of the dwellings concerned. However, landlords felt that it would not be fair on other tenants or neighbours to let to families because of the potential for greater disturbance. Other landlords stressed the cost element due to increased wear and tear on property. However, a small number of landlords suggested they preferred families because they felt they were more stable than other types of tenant and were more likely to have a responsible attitude.

A formal sideline landlord tried to let to families for this reason:

> We try to let to families if possible. I suppose you tend to think the families with children are more reliable because obviously their children need a decent home and...well, you just hope that they're going to be more reliable.

Research has shown that the economic status of tenants is important to landlords. Most landlords prefer employed people to tenants out of work (Kemp and Rhodes, 1994a, 1994b; Crook *et al*, 1995). Many respondents mentioned that they would much prefer to see employed tenants in their properties. One managing agent suggested that:

> Where we are letting or re-letting what I am looking for is Mr and Mrs Average. I do not want DSS. I do not want unemployed. I do not want problems. Enough problems evolve without walking into them to start with.

A couple of landlords suggested that they would rather let to the homeless if they were in some form of employment, than to unemployed people.

There appeared to be a difference between respondents' actual and preferred letting strategies. Many landlords commented that whilst they could still generally fill vacancies quite quickly, they were finding it harder to find 'good' or preferred tenants. It was felt that one reason for this was the increase in the supply of dwellings in the private rented sector. Some landlords found that they were increasingly accepting tenants that they would prefer not to let to, including tenants on Housing Benefit.

A business landlord felt that:

> And I mean in the B&B accommodation we've only had three working people. One of them was an architect who kept falling down into alcoholism. I prefer working people in flats if I can get them, but again, it's not easy.

The 'ideal' tenant

Many landlords felt that they were looking for qualities in people which they felt would make them 'good' tenants. The qualities described as desirable by landlords reflected a range of concerns about letting property. In many instances, landlords stated that ideally they just wanted tenants who would fulfill their contractual obligations with regard to the payment of rent and bills. A number of landlords also mentioned that they wanted tenants who would look after the property and keep it clean. As a formal sideline landlord put it,

> *Somebody who keeps the house clean and tidy, and pays the rent on time. That's all I ask really. I don't want any more than that.*

Some landlords also stated a number of personal attributes which they felt were important, such as the ability to get on with other tenants, and having a polite and responsible attitude. In particular, many resident landlords emphasised that ideally they were looking for tenants they could get on with.

A number of landlords commented that they would not want to let to people whose appearance suggested that they would not meet these expectations. This included people who were dirty, appeared violent, particularly alcoholics and anybody involved in drugs. Whilst most landlords were careful to stress their lack of prejudice when choosing tenants, it was clear that there were a small number who would turn people down on grounds of race.

Previous research has suggested that an overwhelming majority of landlords do not want to let to people on Housing Benefit, or do not have a preference either way (Kemp and Rhodes, 1994a, 1994b). The attitudes of landlords in this study suggested accordance with these findings. There was a fairly even split between those landlords who would prefer not to let to tenants on Housing Benefit, and those who said they did not mind. Business landlords and agents were more amenable to accepting tenants on Housing Benefit. However, agents tended to stress that the majority of their client landlords did not want tenants on Housing Benefit.

A commonly shared view among respondents who did not express a preference was that the source of a tenant's income was irrelevant, as long as the rent was paid. Previous research has found a variety of reasons why many landlords do not want to let to tenants on Housing Benefit. These are mainly concerned with difficulties surrounding the administration of Housing Benefit; the undesirable image which a number of landlords have about tenants on Housing Benefit; and the financially insecure position of the people receiving such payments (Kemp and Rhodes, 1994a, 1994b; Crook *et al*, 1995). The opinions of landlords in this study who did not want to let to tenants on Housing Benefit tended to focus on these issues. A number of respondents differentiated between what they saw as the general behaviour of tenants on Housing Benefit and other tenants. Many landlords also commented that they had experienced difficulties with the administration of Housing Benefit. These are discussed in the next chapter.

A small number of business landlords and an agent stated that they preferred to let to tenants on Housing Benefit. These landlords took great care over the types of tenant they would accept, with an emphasis on characteristics such as stability and long-lasting tenancies. As part of this letting strategy, Housing Benefit was viewed as a stable and guaranteed form of income.

It has been suggested that the current arrangements for the protection of vulnerable groups allows landlords to target these groups and charge higher rents in the knowledge that local authorities will find it harder to restrict benefit (DSS, 1995).

Very little evidence was found in the research to suggest that respondents in general had enough knowledge of the rules governing protected groups to be in a position to take advantage of them. Most sideline landlords were not aware of the regulations concerning vulnerable groups and most did not know that a distinction was made between different types of tenant. Business landlords and agents were more likely to know about protected groups, although in some instances this seemed more intuitive than based on a knowledge of the actual legislation. For example, one business landlord said that he thought that lone parent families were probably viewed more sympathetically by the local authority than other types of tenant.

However, knowledge of the legislation with respect to vulnerable groups did not mean that landlords were actively targeting these types of tenant for that reason. One landlord felt that it would be possible to target lone parent families on Housing Benefit, although as a preference, he would rather let to people in employment. Virtually all of his tenants were in work.

Selecting tenants

A distinction can be made between the general preferences of landlords and the process of actually selecting a tenant. Many respondents commented that they often relied upon 'gut reaction' when they met prospective tenants, and were looking for individuals whom they felt would make 'good' tenants. A number of respondents emphasised that they were concerned about the character and physical appearance of the person involved: their personality; demeanour and dress. As one landlord put it:

> You try and become a judge of character and just take it on that. We look
> at them and if they seem presentable and they've got good manners about
> them - you take it on appearances and that's it really isn't it?

Some landlords letting shared accommodation commented that an important consideration in choosing tenants was whether they would fit into the dynamics of an existing household and be able to get on with other tenants. Unusually, one resident landlord stated that this was a particular concern, and on average spent two to three months choosing tenants to fill vacancies. Other landlords commented that an important consideration was the character of the neighbourhood where properties were located, as well as the neighbours themselves. For example, an agent suggested that he would not place students in certain areas because of the possibility of friction with other residents.

Respondents commented that, in spite of their efforts when choosing tenants, in practice it was very difficult to predict how a person would behave in a tenancy until they had moved in. One strategy to get around this uncertainty which was favoured by a number of sideline landlords was to try and let to people they knew. One landlord felt that friends and relatives were more reliable as tenants than people they did not know. Resident landlords in particular often let to a friend or acquaintance. Another strategy adopted by a business landlord was to use six month assured shorthold tenancies as a form of probationary tenancy.

A number of landlords stated that their choice of tenant was constrained by the attitude of insurance companies towards certain types of tenant. One managing agent suggested that many of his client landlords could not let to people out of work, or to students, because clauses in their insurance policies specifically debarred landlords from letting to these groups of people. A couple of landlords said they had experienced considerable difficulty in getting their property insured.

Rent ceilings and letting strategies

From October 1995, Housing Benefit for dwellings in the deregulated private sector will be calculated with regard to local reference rents (see chapter one). The willingness of landlords to let to tenants on Housing Benefit could be affected by these changes. At the time of the fieldwork, press stories had suggested that rent ceilings might be introduced (which are not the same as reference rents). The interviews therefore explored the attitudes of landlords to these.

Many respondents felt that they were unsure how a rent ceiling might affect their letting preferences until the changes actually came into effect. However, a number of landlords anticipated that the impact on their personal letting strategies would depend on the calculation of a rent ceiling for an area in relation to what they, as landlords, considered to be market rents. Some respondents commented that if the ceilings were too low for their own personal requirements then they would probably not let to tenants on Housing

Benefit. A couple of landlords stated that their ability to continue as landlords depended on a certain return and if this was not forthcoming then they would have no choice but not to let to tenants on Housing Benefit. A formal sideline landlord felt that:

> It would give guidelines on what to go for as well. If I thought I can get £65 a week off there, but I needed £80, I would just be wasting my time really, wouldn't I, because it wouldn't pay for itself.

One formal sideline landlord stated that in the light of the current proposals he was already thinking about changing the type of tenant he generally let to and reducing the number of tenants on Housing Benefit. A business landlord suggested that if the ceiling was at the level of his current rents then this would be an incentive to let to people on Housing Benefit. If, however, he considered that a ceiling was too low then he would ask prospective tenants on Housing Benefit to make up the difference themselves before allowing them into the property.

Many informal sideline landlords felt the introduction of a ceiling would make it more difficult for tenants on Housing Benefit to find good quality accommodation in the private rented sector and suggested that there was a danger of such tenants being excluded from tenancies.

Pre-tenancy determinations

NACAB (1990) and others (Kemp et al, 1994) have drawn attention to the difficulty faced by tenants of having to enter into rental agreements without knowing whether Housing Benefit will cover the rent expected. The introduction of pre-tenancy determinations (see chapter one) will give tenants and their landlords an indication of the likely rent that will be eligible for Housing Benefit.

There was a general feeling among landlords that the introduction of pre-tenancy determinations would be an improvement to the present system. One agent considered that it would reduce an element of risk for landlords in accepting people claiming Housing Benefit in that they would be aware of the likely figure they could receive. He felt that this would mean that landlords would be in a better position to judge whether Housing Benefit would meet their requirements, particularly where mortgage repayments and other loans had to be covered.

However, a number of landlords expressed concern that, whilst this might be good for them, it could have an adverse effect upon people relying on Housing Benefit:

If the landlord didn't think it was a fair rent they could let it to somebody else who was willing to pay the rent. It wouldn't be very good for the people on the DSS though.

Likewise, several sideline landlords felt that, if the amount was too low, then they would probably not accept tenants on Housing Benefit. One sideline landlord stated that if the decision was slightly lower than the amount he expected, then he would be prepared to lower the rent. However, if he felt the difference was too great, then he would not accept tenants on Housing Benefit. An agent felt that knowledge of the amount of rent that Housing Benefit might cover would be helpful in encouraging landlords to accept tenants on Housing Benefit as a last resort if other types of tenant could not be found.

Whilst many landlords felt that they would welcome the introduction of pre-tenancy certificates, there may be a significant difference between the sort of scheme they might prefer and the actual scheme that is to be introduced. The current proposals envisage a service primarily for tenants. Landlords will not be in a position to take advantage of the service themselves, unless the request is linked to a claim by a tenant for Housing Benefit.

Whether landlords would accept homeless households

The government's published proposals on access to social housing (DoE, 1994) has envisaged much greater use being made of the private rented sector by local authorities to house the homeless. Landlords' attitudes to this issue are therefore very important.

A number of business landlords and agents were already letting accommodation to homeless households on behalf of statutory and voluntary agencies. Respondents were involved for a number of reasons. Most landlords and agents said they were motivated by a concern for the predicament of homeless people and felt that they were in a position to do something practical to alleviate the problem in their local area. Allied to this view was the feeling that landlords were providing a service as well as running a business. This was reflected in the comments of a few landlords who felt there was an element of 'social work' in their role as landlords. In addition, there was the opinion that accommodation for homeless households could be provided which achieved a commercial return but which was also efficient and cost-effective.

Many landlords suggested that they did not want to become involved in accepting homeless households or were very wary of the idea. A commonly held view was that if they did become involved then they would want to be able to choose carefully and retain strict control over accepting a tenant into their property. One landlord thought that:

I'd consider that, but I think it would only be fair to the tenants on either side, to vet the people before I let them in. I'd want to know who they were and what they were about, because it's easy for me as a landlord to say 'Yes, that's a great idea'. I live four miles away from the house we're talking about. But I think it's morally wrong to just say, 'right put a problem family there' - if we're talking problem families - and let the neighbours suffer.

Some landlords did not see any reason why they should accept homeless households at all, and saw this as the duty of local authorities and central government. A number suggested that there should be an increase in provision by local housing authorities.

A number of landlords had negative perceptions of people who were homeless. Some landlords felt that it would not be fair on other tenants or neighbours to accept homeless households. One landlord went so far as to suggest that a separate building would have to be provided which was specially sound-proofed.

One reason for the wariness evident amongst a number of landlords could be that many of them automatically associated the issue of housing homeless households from local authorities with families rather than other household types. It has already been shown that many landlords prefer not to let to families with children. Some landlords tended to be dismissive of the idea of providing accommodation for homeless households in general, because they felt that the accommodation they were providing was not suitable for families.

Any reduction in the supply of dwellings for rent could have an impact upon the attitudes of landlords remaining on the sector. A number of landlords considered that they would only let to homeless households as a last resort, if they could not find 'preferred' tenants. Other landlords stated that they were only letting to tenants on benefits because of the current balance of supply and demand between rented dwellings and prospective tenants.

Some landlords who were not already involved in letting to homeless households expressed an interest in doing so. This was mainly amongst other business landlords and agents, although a number of sideline landlords thought that they would like to become involved.

One business landlord and a formal sideline landlord felt that they would seriously consider becoming involved in such an arrangement if grants were available to renovate properties. The respondents suggested that they would be prepared to invest in property for this purpose with the aid of grants. There was a strong feeling that landlords could play a useful role in partnership with local authorities in reducing waiting lists for council accommodation and bringing disused property back into use. One landlord who was already involved in housing homeless households stressed the positive incentive of receiving renovation grants in return for nomination rights as a means of furthering his business.

A few landlords expressed interest in leasing properties to local authorities or housing associations. This was seen as a 'hassle-free' way of letting. A formal sideline landlord suggested that he had become disillusioned with letting accommodation as a result of experiences with 'problem' tenants and was also concerned that a couple of his properties were in 'unsafe' areas. He viewed the possibility of leasing to a housing association as a means of offloading the management side of the business without having to sell his portfolio. In another instance, a formal sideline landlord saw this as a means of helping homeless households but with the responsibility for the maintenance of the tenancies and property resting firmly with the managing agent.

A number of landlords thought that one of the main advantages to them of accepting homeless households was that the rental income would be virtually guaranteed by Housing Benefit. However, there was concern over the way Housing Benefit was administered. An agent who was already involved in a scheme stated that their biggest problem with homeless households was with the administration of Housing Benefit. He stated that one household formerly registered as homeless with a local authority had been evicted as a result of problems with Housing Benefit payments.

The ability of the private rented sector to meet the new demands being placed upon it in terms of housing the homeless could depend on the robustness of its revival evident in recent years. It has been suggested that since many of the properties currently available for rent are the result of the state of the owner occupied property market, any improvement in the market could see a sharp fall in the supply of dwellings available for homeless households. Crook *et al* (1995) have estimated that if house prices rose whilst rent levels remained stable, then the number of lettings owned by current landlords would fall by about one fifth. Some landlords who expressed interest in housing the homeless were only letting their properties because they felt they could not sell in the current market. One landlord only let either to close friends and relatives, or to people in his local community who were homeless. However, he described himself as a reluctant landlord and would sell as soon as the market picked up.

Summary

The main findings to emerge in this chapter were:

▸   Most landlords said they did not have a preference as to the type of person they wanted when they were looking for tenants. Instead, most respondents concerned about looking for characteristics which they felt would make people 'good' tenants.

▶   Many landlords commented that they did not want to let to young single people, or to people out of work. Attitudes to letting to other types of tenant were mixed.

▶   Landlords generally did not want to let to tenants on Housing Benefit, or said that they did not have a preference.

▶   Many respondents were unsure about how the introduction of rent ceilings and pre-tenancy certificates might affect their letting strategies until the changes actually came into effect. A number of respondents expressed apprehension about the impact of the changes on the ability of people on Housing Benefit to gain access to accommodation.

▶   Most sideline landlords tended to be very wary about accepting homeless households as tenants. However, many business landlords and agents were already actively involved in housing homeless households, or expressed interest in the idea.

Chapter Six
Experience of Housing Benefit Administration

Introduction

Previous research has highlighted a number of problems with the administration of Housing Benefit (NACAB, 1990; Audit Commission; 1993). This chapter therefore focuses upon landlords' experiences of the administration of the scheme. In particular, it examines the time taken to process Housing Benefit claims, the problem for landlords of tenants moving on before their claim is processed, the payment of Housing Benefit direct to landlords, the recovery of overpayments, and dealing with the Housing Benefit office.

Delays in processing claims

One of the difficulties identified with the administration of Housing Benefit has been the length of time it can take to process a claim. Local authorities have a duty to make the first payment of Housing Benefit within fourteen days of receiving a claim, or, if that is not reasonably practicable, as soon as possible thereafter. Sharp (1991) has suggested that delays in the processing of claims above this period have caused problems between landlords and tenants in the private rented sector.

A couple of sideline landlords said that they had not experienced any problems with delays. One landlord stated that whilst there had been a problem with delays in the past, claims were now processed in about two weeks. However, most landlords cited delays as one of the main problems they experienced with tenants on Housing Benefit. Sideline landlords felt that one to two months was the average amount of time that they had to wait for a claim to be processed, whilst business landlords and agents suggested that about two to three months was the norm. Many landlords could cite examples where they had to wait far longer for individual claims to be processed. The most extreme example was a wait of about two years.

Some landlords recognised that a reason for delay was that tenants had given insufficient information in pursuit of their claim. However, there was a general feeling amongst many respondents that delays were due to a failing in the way that Housing Benefit was administered.

I think they have an obligation to deal with the application within 14 days if all the paperwork is there, but the trick is if all the paperwork isn't there, then of course there's no need to deal with it and of course they can't deal with it, I appreciate that. But I know over the years of many cases where the paperwork has been there and has been in the file, its just that the file hasn't been adequately dealt with.

A number of respondents stated that they were prepared to wait for claims to be processed in the knowledge that they would eventually come through and that any arrears would be paid off in the first back-dated payment. One landlord commented that once the initial period of waiting was over, Housing Benefit seemed to *'tick along'* without much further trouble.

However, other landlords employed particular strategies to cope with delays in Housing Benefit payments. One business landlord tried to speed up the process by writing to the Housing Benefit office, threatening to evict the tenant in question unless the claim could be processed more rapidly. At the same time, the landlord gave assurances to the tenant that this was just a ploy to try and reduce the delay in the processing of the claim. Other landlords expected tenants to actively pursue their claim and find out the reason for the delay. Some landlords took this responsibility upon themselves and tried to liaise with Housing Benefit offices to reduce delays. Another business landlord responded to delays in the processing of claims for Housing Benefit by complaining to the Ombudsman about his local authority, who were subsequently found guilty of maladministration. A couple of landlords had responded to their experiences of dealing with the Housing Benefit system by not accepting any more tenants on Housing Benefit. Both respondents shared the view that this was unfair on people who relied on Housing Benefit, but they felt that the way Housing Benefit was administered was too inefficient.

A number of landlords felt that whilst delays were inconvenient, they could draw upon other sources of income or 'make do' until Housing Benefit was paid. In a number of instances, sideline landlords stated that their tenants had managed to pay the rent from their own resources, whilst waiting for the claim to be processed. One sideline landlord employed the tactic of not accepting any tenants who were claiming Housing Benefit unless they agreed to pay the rent from their own resources whilst waiting for the claim to be processed.

Other respondents stressed that the temporary loss of rental income was problematic for them. In a number of instances it was clear that delays had caused financial hardship for some landlords. One sideline landlord had incurred bank charges by taking out an overdraft to cover the interrupted income. A couple of agents emphasised the difficulty that delays placed upon client landlords who had to cover mortgage repayments. One agent tried to alleviate the problem for these client landlords by passing on the deposit to help with mortgage repayments, although the agent would only do this if he was sure that Housing Benefit would eventually be paid. A couple of business landlords felt that they were being asked to subsidise tenants on Housing Benefit whilst their claims were being processed.

A number of landlords with small portfolios expressed anxiety about having more than one tenant claiming Housing Benefit at the same time. One sideline landlord had found that a number of tenants in his property had been trying to claim Housing Benefit at the same time, and that delays on these claims had resulted in substantial arrears. A couple of sideline landlords also expressed concern over the stress and anxiety that delays in payment of Housing Benefit had caused their tenants.

Tenants moving out before a claim had been processed

A number of landlords highlighted the issue of tenants moving out of property before a claim for Housing Benefit had been processed. This seemed to be mainly a problem for business landlords and agents, although a number of sideline landlords also had experience of this. Many landlords stated that they did not receive any payment of rent from tenants until a claim for Housing Benefit had been successfully processed. If a tenant moved out before a claim for Housing Benefit had been dealt with, this could be a source of potential difficulty for landlords. The tenant might be found to be ineligible for Housing Benefit, or the Housing Benefit office may require further information from the tenant before the claim could be processed.

For a number of landlords this potential difficulty had been resolved satisfactorily and either Housing Benefit had been paid for the period in which the tenant had been resident, or the tenant themselves had subsequently found the resources to pay the arrears.

However, other landlords stated that their experiences of this had been more problematic, either because a tenant had been found to be not eligible for Housing Benefit, or because the tenant had not supplied all the correct information to the Housing Benefit office before they had moved out. A couple of landlords also stated that Housing Benefit offices had lost the application forms of tenants who had moved out, and had required fresh claims to be made from tenants who were no longer present in the tenancy. The problem was compounded by the fact that many respondents found that it was very difficult to trace the whereabouts of former tenants, either to try and recover arrears from them, or to ask them to supply the required information to the Housing Benefit office to enable a claim to be processed.

Some landlords tried to minimise the risk of losing money when tenants had moved out before a claim had been processed. A couple of landlords maintained regular visits to each property to check if tenants were still present. Other respondents tried to ensure that all the correct information necessary for a claim was in the hands of the Housing Benefit office. Landlords employing this tactic met with mixed success. Some landlords stated that they had experienced difficulty in trying to liaise with Housing Benefit offices, and found the attitude of many staff very unhelpful.

Direct payments of Housing Benefit

Many landlords felt that one of the positive features of the Housing Benefit system was the ability to have Housing Benefit payments sent direct. It was felt that this simplified the process of rent collection and saved a great deal of time and effort. Many landlords also felt that most tenants preferred Housing Benefit to be sent direct as it meant that they did not have to worry about paying the rent themselves.

However, a number of landlords commented that they did not feel that having Housing Benefit sent direct was particularly important for them and left this decision to the tenant. Other landlords felt that Housing Benefit should be sent to tenants on principle. There was a view that payment direct to the landlord encouraged a 'culture of dependency' and implied that tenants could not be trusted with their own finances.

Most landlords said that they preferred or insisted on Housing Benefit being sent direct to them. To a certain extent, this reflected the attitude of a number of respondents that Housing Benefit was *their* rent money and was not viewed as a benefit to tenants to help cover housing costs. Many landlords who asked for Housing Benefit to be sent direct said they had previously experienced difficulty in obtaining the rent from tenants on Housing Benefit.

A common experience among landlords seemed to be for a tenant to have had Housing Benefit sent to themselves and then to have either built up arrears having spent the money on items other than rent or to have vacated the property altogether. It was experiences like this that had led many landlords to insist on the Housing Benefit being paid directly to them.

A particular problem mentioned by a number of respondents was for a tenant to vacate a property having received a large backdated payment of Housing Benefit caused by delays in the processing of a claim. A landlord highlighted the practice of one local authority, which was to send the first payment of Housing Benefit direct to the landlord in an attempt to get around this problem.

A number of landlords felt that allowing Housing Benefit payments to be made to tenants was a weakness in the current legislation and that Housing Benefit sent direct to landlords should be made mandatory. In a number of instances landlords tried to ensure that rent direct was compulsory for tenants, by making this part of the letting agreement. Tenants trying to redirect Housing Benefit to themselves would be served with a notice to quit, or would not have their tenancy renewed.

Overpayments

An agent commented that receiving payments of housing benefit direct was double edged for landlords because of the possibility of overpayments. Where an overpayment has occurred and the benefit was paid directly to the landlord, it is the landlord that has responsibility for repaying the excess.

Business landlords and agents in particular identified the recovery of overpayments as a source of difficulty for them. Respondents identified two potential causes of overpayments. Firstly overpayments could result from a tenant vacating a property, with or without the landlord's knowledge. Sometimes Housing Benefit continued to be paid until the Housing Benefit office were notified. Many landlords stated that if they knew that a tenant had left, then overpayments tended not to be a problem because they could take account of the ineligible payments. However, a number of landlords stated that occasionally they did not know that a tenant had left, and this could cause an unexpected repayment of revenue if ineligible rent was subsequently recovered by the Housing Benefit office.

Secondly, a number of landlords commented that overpayments could also occur if a tenant was not entitled to the amount of Housing Benefit they were being paid. This situation could arise if a tenant in receipt of Housing Benefit took up employment without declaring this to the Housing Benefit office. A number of landlords felt that the system of recovering overpayments from the landlord made them financially responsible for the behaviour of their tenants. One managing agent felt that:

> I can't control whether the guy signs on or not, whether he loses Income Support or not, because the DSS doesn't write to me. I don't get that information, hence I can't do anything about it

In particular there was a view that it was unfair to 'punish' the landlord if a tenant had broken the law by taking on undeclared work whilst claiming benefit.

Some landlords tried to minimise the possibility of overpayments by employing a variety of strategies. A number of landlords maintained regular visits to properties to check if tenants had moved out. A couple of respondents stated that if they found out that a tenant had taken up undeclared work then they would give them a few days to declare this before reporting them to the Housing Benefit office.

A couple of agents commented on the financial difficulty overpayments had caused them. They said that often the money had been sent on to the landlord before they knew that the money would be recovered by the Housing Benefit office. The agents incurred losses as they found it hard to recover money from either the landlords or the tenants involved. A number of landlords also mentioned that it was difficult to recover rent arrears from tenants, particularly if they had left the property. One landlord commented that overpayments had caused financial difficulty as the rent was needed to cover the repayment of a mortgage.

Dealing with the Housing Benefit office

If greater use is to be made of the private rented sector by local authorities, then this will require a closer working relationship between landlords and local authorities, including Housing Benefit offices. This part of the chapter explores current attitudes and experiences of landlords to Housing Benefit offices.

Many sideline landlords who let on an informal basis had very little contact with Housing Benefit offices. A small number of them felt that relations with the Housing Benefit office were very constructive and did not suggest there were any real problems. However, other sideline landlords, as well as business landlords and agents, were more negative about their experiences of dealing with Housing Benefit offices. There was a general perception among these respondents that Housing Benefit offices were very obstructive and uncooperative towards landlords.

Some landlords expressed frustration at their inability to gain information about the status of a tenant's claim. Given the lengthy delays in processing some claims, they felt that they should have a right to know how long they would have to wait or whether the tenant would be eligible for Housing Benefit. One business landlord felt that the processing of Housing Benefit claims effectively relied on the goodwill of landlords to suspend the rental agreement between the landlord and tenant.

A number of landlords felt that, in their experience, it was not the staff of Housing Benefit offices which were at fault, but that the system of Housing Benefit did not seem to be very efficient. However, some business landlords and agents who had tenancies which crossed local authority boundaries commented that there was a marked difference in the attitudes and working practices of the various authorities they had contact with. One agent stated that dealing with the Housing Benefit office had improved dramatically since their local authority had appointed a Landlord Liaison Officer to work with landlords.

Summary

The main findings to emerge in this chapter were:

- Most respondents had experienced problems with letting to tenants on Housing Benefit. Many landlords cited delays in the processing of claims as one of the principal difficulties they had experienced.

- Landlords highlighted the issue of tenants moving out of a property before a claim for Housing Benefit had been processed, which often left the landlord with unpaid rent and no Housing Benefit for the period when the tenant was living in the accommodation

- Housing Benefit paid direct to the landlord was seen as a positive feature of the Housing Benefit system as it meant they were guaranteed to receive the rent

- But landlords were unhappy that they were obliged to return overpaid Housing Benefit where it had been paid directly to them but they had received no more than the rent that was due

- There was a view that Housing Benefit offices were generally unsupportive of, and unsympathetic to, private landlords

Chapter Seven
Setting the Rent

Introduction

This chapter examines landlords' and agents' attitudes and approaches to setting the rent for their accommodation. It looks at how they decide what rent to charge, whether they ever negotiate the rent with tenants, and whether they charge the same or a different rent to people who are on Housing Benefit from the rent that they charge to other tenants. The chapter also reports on whether landlords and agents were aware that the rent officer service is involved in the Housing Benefit scheme and, if they were, whether they took the rent officer into account when setting the rent for their accommodation. Finally, the chapter examines whether landlords and agents were aware that rents could be restricted for Housing Benefit assessment purposes and how they had responded, or how they thought they would respond, to restrictions in their own tenants' rent.

Deciding the rent

There were important differences between landlords in the ways in which they went about setting the rent. *Informal sideline* landlords were the least likely to be influenced by the lettings market in deciding what to charge for their accommodation. Most informal sideline landlords did seek out evidence of market rents locally, mainly by consulting newspapers but in some cases by asking what the prospective tenants had paid in their previous accommodation. A few informal landlords asked their tenants what rent they thought the landlord should charge. Some set the rent at a level that covered their outgoings - in particular, their mortgage costs but also other bills - and paid little attention to market rent evidence.

Among the *formal sideline* landlords, some simply relied on the letting agent to come up with a figure; though one did this for the first tenancy only and thereafter decided the rent himself, using evidence on market rents. Some formal sideline landlords had a minimum figure - a reserve rent, as it were - which covered their outgoings, below which they did not want to fall; in most of these cases this reserve rent was then checked against market evidence from newspapers and other sources.

Quite a few formal sideline landlords said simply that they set the rent based on what other landlords were charging for similar properties in the local area (again, mainly using newspaper advertisements as the prime source of information). As one of them put it,

> *I arrived at the rent level by looking at what other people were charging for similar accommodation, knowing that the house had been nicely done up.*

Some of these landlords deliberately set the rent at a bit below what they calculated was the market level, though one only did this for what he perceived to be good tenants. The rationale for this strategy was that they hoped that a below market rent would encourage the tenant to stay for a long time, thereby reducing the risk of having a property standing empty, with all of the loss in rent and risk of vandalism that that implied. Thus these landlords were turnover minimisers rather than rent maximisers.

> *Well I know basically what the level of rent is around here, and I try to ask for a market rent. But if I think that the tenant might be a good one I would rather charge less and just keep that tenant happy. Because it is no good trying to ask a very high rent to which the tenant agrees but is out after two months, and you have to start again. So that's my attitude to rent.*

Finally, one sideline landlord who had not approached letting as a business venture but who needed to cover certain costs, asked the current tenant how much Housing Benefit she was likely to receive and then set the rent in line with that amount.

As the term we have used suggests, *business* landlords were much more businesslike in their approach to rent setting. All of them looked at what other landlords were charging for equivalent properties in the local area. Even so, several said they pitched the rent a bit below the market level in order to reduce the risk of tenant turnover. Two said that, as well as market evidence, they took into account what the rent officer decides in making determinations for Housing Benefit purposes.

All of the *agents* said they based the rent on market evidence using their extensive day to day letting experience and taking into account the location, type and (less often mentioned) the condition of the property. As one of them put it, *'It's what market forces dictate; at the end of the day what people will pay'*. Only one agent sought to pitch the rent below the market level, in order to minimise tenant turnover. Most of the agents stressed that they had to abide by the instructions of their client landlords; and while some of their clients left it pretty much to the agent to decide upon the rent, others had rents in mind which they wanted to be charged.

Negotiating the rent?

Most *informal sideline* landlords said they would be prepared to negotiate with the prospective tenant over the rent level. One such landlord said she much preferred the tenant to suggest a figure. Another said she checked with the tenant whether the rent she was asking for was too high, though she remarked that people on Housing Benefit did not care about the rent level.

Many *formal sideline* landlords said that the rent was fixed; that they would not negotiate with the tenant over the rent level as they had to cover their costs (and in particular, their mortgage). One formal sideline landlord said he did not like to negotiate and was always suspicious of a prospective tenant who asked for a lower rent than the amount asked: *'It would always be a great danger signal to me, if somebody said "Its a bit steep for me. Can we say £130?"'* Others said that they would negotiate the rent if necessary and one always did so:

> *Yes, I always negotiate the rent. I propose what I think the rent should be, and we just have a quiet chat and come to some kind of agreement....its no good asking some fantastic figure if I know the tenant cannot pay it....Nobody is going to gain.*

Most *business* landlords were prepared to negotiate over the rent level, at least to some extent. A minority said that the rent was fixed or that they tried to avoid negotiation if they could; they did so only on rare occasions to prevent the property from standing empty.

Most of the *agents* whom we interviewed said that they would negotiate over rent levels and some had actually done so. Some of these agents said that this was inevitable, while others said it was better to have some rent than none at all. *'I mean the rents are flexible. Its whether or not you can let the property, that's the main thing'.*

One agent said that he quite commonly had to negotiate over rents, but that only rarely did a tenant on Housing Benefit ask for a reduction in the rent. In contrast, another agent, who had been approached on a number of occasions by tenants who wanted to have the rent reduced, said that it usually occurred when the Housing Benefit had been restricted. How this latter agent dealt with such requests, he said, depended on the landlord, but 90 per cent would not agree to reduce it.

Two managing agents said they would definitely not reduce the rent. This was because landlords needed to make a return and, anyway, they were already charging a market rent. But even one of these agents said he might take a lenient view if a tenant wanted to negotiate a lower rent because of a change of circumstances.

Higher rents for tenants on HB?

Most of the *informal sideline* landlords said they charged the same rent to people on Housing Benefit as to those in work. It made no difference to them whether the tenant was on Housing Benefit or not, they stressed, so long as the rent was paid. One informal sideline landlord had actually reduced the rent from £60 to £40 per week when the tenant had become unemployed and had to claim Housing Benefit. In contrast, two informal landlords said they had charged more to someone on Housing Benefit. In one case this was because the rent was not being paid out of the tenant's income. In the other case, the landlord claimed that the tenant had asked him to state that the rent was higher than he was actually charging, in order to help him out.

Almost all of the *formal sideline* landlords said that they charged the same rents; they made no distinction between those on benefit and those who were not. Many landlords took the question to mean, did they charge a *lower* rent to someone because they were on Housing Benefit; and responded by saying that they were unwilling or not in a financial position to be able to do that. *'I really can't afford to differentiate'.*

One formal sideline landlord reported that he had charged the previous tenant, who had been working, more than the current tenant who was on Housing Benefit. Another said that all tenants start on the same rent, but if a tenant subsequently went onto Housing Benefit they would just charge what the Housing Benefit office would pay, which was usually a bit less than he was charging people in work.

All but one of the *business* landlords said they charged the same rent to all their tenants irrespective of whether they were on Housing Benefit or not. One business landlord reported that he felt he usually ended up losing slightly if the tenant was on Housing Benefit. Another landlord stated that he sets a fair market rent and he expected to get it; if the rent was restricted, he expected the tenant to make up the difference; hence he would not agree to a *lower* rent just because someone was in receipt of Housing Benefit.

One business landlord did admit to charging more to people on Housing Benefit. Originally, he used to charge the same amount, but now added £5 per week to cover the problems and hassle incurred in the process of getting the Housing Benefit. He felt that tenants were not bothered about the rent because they were not paying it for themselves.

Likewise, all but one of the *managing agents* said that they charged the same rent. Many stressed that there was no reason why they should differentiate between tenants on Housing Benefit and those who were not. The rent was based on the market, not on the personal circumstances of the tenant.

One agent had two lists of accommodation as some landlords took only people in work, others only those on Housing Benefit, while other landlords had no preference. It was clear from these lists that, among those who took both, many had two rent figures, with the higher one for Housing Benefit claimants. This list was shown to one of the researchers by the agent's secretary.

Awareness of the rent officer

More than half of the *informal sideline* landlords were aware that the rent officer existed - or as one respondent described them, *'someone who was not the council'* - and might visit to inspect the property, to check whether or not the rent was reasonable. Inevitably, the degree of knowledge about the rent officer's precise duties varied considerably between these respondents, but all of them had some idea of what the rent officer did in respect of Housing Benefit claims. This information was not always complete and in one case it was rather inaccurate, the landlord being under the impression that the rent officer could restrict the contractual rent and insist that the landlord bring their property up to standard and install such things as central heating: *'So he sounds like quite a guy this rent officer'*.

In some cases, the landlord became aware of the rent officer's role in the scheme because they had visited the property to make an inspection, though they apparently did not always explain who they were or why they had come. As one resident landlord put it: *'Somebody came round, who didn't say who he was. He got out a tape measure and started walking round the house'*. Nevertheless, a substantial minority of informal sideline landlords had neither heard of the rent officer nor were aware that they were involved in the administration of the scheme.

Most *formal sideline* landlords knew about the rent officer or at the least that someone would or could check the property to see if the rent was reasonable. Again, some respondents were unclear or hazy about the details of the rent officer's involvement in the scheme.

All of the *business* landlords were aware that the rent officers had a role in checking whether the rent being charged was reasonable or not. One business landlord felt that he had a good relationship - and, indeed, a good reputation - with the rent officer and had quite a lot of contact with them professionally. Two thirds to three quarters of this landlord's tenants were on Housing Benefit.

Like the business landlords, all of the *managing agents* knew that the rent officer had some kind of role in Housing Benefit. Some of the agents were very well informed about this, but others had a more limited knowledge. It was agents who had a relatively sizeable amount of Housing Benefit tenants who had a good knowledge, and those with relatively few tenants on Housing Benefit who had a poor knowledge, of the rent officer's role. One agent reported that rent officers picked up rental lists from them for guidance about rental values in the area.

> ...the rent officer comes round once or twice a year; he looks at the papers and at advertisements and he goes to local agents to form an opinion of what a fair market rent will be.

Was the rent officer taken into account in setting rents?

Quite obviously, among formal and informal sideline landlords, those who were unaware of the rent officer's role in the Housing Benefit scheme did not take them into account when setting the rent. However, almost all of the *informal sideline* landlords who were aware of the rent officer said that they did not take them into account when setting the rent. One landlord said she was aware that the rent should not seem excessive, so it is possible that she implicitly if not explicitly bore the rent officer's role in mind when setting the rent. Another said that if the rent officer's figure was lower than hers, she would drop it to that amount.

Most of the *formal sideline* landlords who knew about the rent officer said they also took no account of them in deciding what rent to charge. But two formal landlords did: one said he tended to be guided by what the Housing Benefit office would pay; the other that she felt she had to keep the rent officer in mind. In both cases, all of their tenants were in receipt of Housing Benefit. Another formal sideline landlord acknowledged that he probably did take the rent officer into account *'without realising it'*, simply because the rent officer's decisions effectively determined what rent they would in practice be able to get from someone on Housing Benefit.

> Yes, I suppose we do really, because we know from the other houses [that we let] more or less what he's going to say, and we know that we're with him, or usually five or ten pounds more than what he assesses. So I suppose we do consider what he's going to say. If we're in an area where we know he's going to come back at, say, sixty pounds a week, we know it's pointless us going and saying, "oh, eighty pounds a week"' if he's going to come back at sixty, really. So, yes, we do take him into account, I suppose.

Some of the *business* landlords stressed that they simply charged what they thought was a market rent and would not ask for less. Other business landlords - all of whom had most or all of their tenants on Housing Benefit - said that they did take the rent officer into account. Thus one business landlord reported that he knew within a few pounds what the rent officer will set, so he rarely got caught out by having a rent restricted. Another stated that he would charge £100 - odd per week if he could get away with it, but that because of the rent officer he knew fine well that he could not get away with it.

Most of the *managing agents* reported that they took no account of the rent officer: they charged a market rent and expected to get it. However, a substantial minority did take at least some account of the rent officer. One such agent, almost all of whose tenants were on Housing Benefit, said that after a while he had got a feel for what the rent officer's figure would be. Another said that, if a prospective tenant was going to be claiming Housing Benefit, he advised the landlord of what could be expected in terms of rents.

Awareness of rent restrictions

Most of the *informal sideline* landlords, even those who were not aware of the rent officer, knew or believed that the rent could be restricted by the Housing Benefit office if the rent was considered to be too high. Most, though, were rather hazy about exactly how this worked. Very few knew anything about the size criteria or the rules on rent increases. Several informal landlords knew nothing about rent restrictions. The knowledge among *formal sideline* landlords was similar to, though in general slightly better than, that of informal landlords.

In contrast to the sideline landlords, all of the *business* landlords knew that the rent could be restricted if it was considered to be too high. And most knew in principle at least, that the rent could be restricted on accommodation size grounds. Indeed, as with managing agents, some business landlords said they tried to match up tenants with the appropriate size of accommodation where they were on Housing Benefit, in order to prevent a rent restriction. Only a few business landlords knew about the rules on reasonable rent increases. One who was aware of these rules remarked that '..*we know fine well that it can only be done once a year*'.

To a greater or lesser degree, all of the *managing agents* were aware that the rent could be restricted by the Housing Benefit office. Most knew it could be restricted if it was considered to be too high; and many also knew about the size criteria. A few knew that rent increases could be restricted. In some cases this knowledge stemmed from actual experience of having the rent restricted by the local authority Housing Benefit office.

Responding to rent restrictions

Experience of rent restrictions was largely confined to business landlords and to the managing agents. None of the informal sideline landlords, and few of the formal sideline landlords, were aware of any of their tenants having had their rent restricted for Housing Benefit purposes. One managing agent said that restrictions varied, with some local authorities restricting rents much more than others. A business landlord said that all of his tenants were automatically restricted by the local authority.

Since the *informal sideline* landlords had no actual experience of restrictions in eligible rents, they were able only to talk hypothetically about how they might respond if it happened to a tenant of theirs. Some were quite clear that they would expect the tenants to make up the difference themselves. *'They'd actually probably move or they'd find the rest of the money themselves.'* One such landlord said she could not afford to accept a lower rent because of the costs she had to meet; another said that if the tenant could not cover the shortfall, she would cut down on the services she provided in order to save money; a third said that, if the tenant could not afford to meet the shortfall, he would negotiate it but might also look for a new tenant.

Other informal sideline landlords felt they would probably accept the reduction; though one of these respondents qualified this by saying that she would only do it if the rent still covered her costs. Several said it would depend, as one of them put it, *'on the margin difference'*. One such informal landlord was not sure how she would deal with a restriction in the rent, but thought that as well as the size of the restriction, it would also depend - echoing a recurrent theme among informal landlords - how well she got on with the tenant; she was more likely to lower the rent if she got on well with the tenant than if she did not. This again illustrates how non-commercial factors entered into the calculations of some informal sideline landlords.

Some of the *formal* sideline landlords were able to talk about how they had actually dealt with rent restrictions they (or rather, their tenants) had had, while others were able to discuss their responses in hypothetical terms only. Either way, the actual or hypothetical responses were not uniform but varied among formal landlords.

Some formal landlords said that the tenant would have to make up the difference themselves or find somewhere else to live. Indeed one landlord always explained in advance to prospective tenants who were on Housing Benefit that if the rent was restricted, they would have to make up the shortfall. A number reported that tenants had always made up the difference (or had left) and that they had never been asked to make a reduction in the rent because it had been restricted by the Housing Benefit office. In those cases the actual amount of the shortfall was always small. One formal sideline landlord, who had reached the point where he was now a reluctant landlord and wished to get rid of his properties, said that the restriction was invariably quite small, *'so we usually just let it go'*, a policy that meant they could avoid *'the turmoil of evicting somebody, which we wouldn't fancy doing. I can't be bothered to do that.'*

Several formal sideline landlords said they would expect the tenant to appeal against a rent restriction. Only a few would lower the rent without having first asked the tenant to put in an appeal. One landlord who required tenants to appeal noted that he had asked tenants to make up the shortfall but that he had found that this was impracticable: they could not afford it.

Among *business* landlords, requiring the tenants to appeal was also a first line of response to rent restrictions in many cases. They reported some success with this strategy, though it did not always work. Perhaps not surprisingly, one such landlord said that, if an appeal was unsuccessful, he would let it go if the shortfall was small but if it was substantial the tenant would have to leave. One landlord said he weighed up whether or not to negotiate a deal with the tenant in order not to have a vacant property or require them to leave. Another said that there was no point in insisting that tenants made up the difference as they could not really afford to do it; so they just had to accept it, for that was the only way to make a living with tenants on Housing Benefit - an unfortunate fact of life. Finally, one formal landlord reported that sometimes he was able to get the shortfall off the tenant, at other times was not able to. He had heart problems and so was not always willing to risk having to go through with the stress that accompanied hassling the tenants for the shortfall.

As with the business landlords, most *managing agents* expected and indeed insisted that the tenant appealed against a rent restriction, a strategy that again was said to be often quite successful. Many also reported that (if the appeal was unsuccessful) they expected the tenant to make up the shortfall. Some of these landlords made the point that if the rent had been negotiated at the outset and the tenant subsequently found that they could not afford it, then they should leave. Many of the agents said that, if arrears developed due to rent restrictions, they would deduct the debt from the tenant's deposit. Only a few agents said that they would negotiate a deal with the tenant and then advise the landlord that a reduced rent was better than an empty property.

Summary

The main findings to emerge in this chapter were as follows:

▸ There was considerable variety in how landlords and agents decided on what rent to charge for their accommodation. Managing agents, most business landlords and some sideline landlords set the rent at the market level. Some business landlords and a few formal landlords deliberately set the rent at below the market level in order to minimise tenant turnover. Some sideline landlords set the rent to cover their costs, while some informal sideline landlords asked the tenant what rent they should charge.

- Most landlords were willing to negotiate the rent with the tenant at the beginning of the tenancy, though far fewer (especially managing agents) were willing to do so once the rent had been agreed and the tenancy commenced.

- Most landlords and agents charged the same rent irrespective of whether or not the tenant was on Housing Benefit. They were not bothered where the rent came from so long as it was paid. But a small minority of respondents did admit to charging a higher rent if the tenant was on Housing Benefit.

- Awareness of the rent officer and rules on rent restrictions in the Housing Benefit system varied. Sideline landlords, especially those operating on an informal basis, were much less likely to be aware of the rent officer or know about the unreasonable rent rates than were business landlords and agents. Business landlords and agents with a high proportion of tenants on Housing Benefit had the most detailed knowledge of the rent officer's role in the scheme and of the unreasonable rent rules.

- Most landlords and agents said they took no account of the rent officer when deciding how much rent to charge, but a minority - all of whom had a high proportion of tenants on Housing Benefit - did take them into account.

- There was great variety in how landlords and agents responded to rent restrictions or how they said they might respond if one of their tenants had their rent restricted. Some would expect the tenant to make up the shortfall themselves or leave; others were prepared to negotiate a deal with the tenant. Many of the more business minded landlords and of the agents insisted, as a first line of response, that the tenant appeal against the restriction, a strategy which was felt to have a high degree of success. Landlords were more likely to let the shortfall go if the restriction was for a small amount.

- Tenants did not always seek to negotiate a lower rent with the landlord if their rent was restricted and some landlords were unaware of whether restrictions had occurred.

Chapter Eight
Conclusions

This final chapter sets out the main conclusions of the research. It seeks to address the research questions set out in chapter one. Before doing so it discusses some important aspects of the characteristics of private landlords because these appear to have an important influence on the way in which landlords operate, their knowledge of the rent officer, and how they have responded, or might respond, to restrictions in eligible rents.

The nature of private landlordism

A key finding of the research, and one which has a bearing on the range of issues examined, is that the respondents were a diverse group of people. The respondents can be considered to form part of a gradation, which consisted of small-scale landlords with very informal arrangements at one extreme, and large well-informed commercially operating businesses at the other. In between these two extremes were people with a variety of business arrangements and outlooks, and varying degrees of knowledge of tenancy law and Housing Benefit regulations.

However, four broad types of respondent were identified in terms of their basic characteristics, what motivated them to become landlords, and how they regarded their portfolios. The four types were the managing agents, business landlords, formally operating sideline landlords, and informally operating sideline landlords.

The letting agents typically performed a complete management service - finding tenants, organising tenancy agreements, and carrying out the day-to-day management of the properties - on behalf of their landlords. The agents generally had the largest portfolios of all the respondents in the survey. Business landlords were full-time private individual landlords, usually having the largest portfolios of the *landlords* who were interviewed, and in a range of shared and sole occupancy lettings. Rental income for their livelihoods was their primary motivation for being landlords, although for some of them this was mitigated by the state of the wider housing market, which had been responsible for rental income assuming importance to them over capital gains. A key characteristic of the business landlords was their emphasis on a continuous process of reinvestment of rental income into the purchase of more property.

The two sub-groups of sideline landlords were not solely, or even primarily, involved with letting their property. Most of them were in full-time paid employment. These landlords were the ones who most commonly had first started letting in 1989 or later. However, their motivations for becoming landlords were not to do with the introduction of the 1988 Housing Act, but commonly because of the slump in the owner occupied housing market, which had made it difficult for them to sell their property. Some of the informally operating sideline landlords in particular, were motivated to let either because they were having difficulties meeting their mortgage repayments, or because they were helping someone out.

Only a few of the landlords had considered, or even given thought to rental income as a return on their capital. Those who had were usually the business landlords. The sideline landlords were mostly concerned that the rental income should cover the costs of their mortgages and other out-goings on their properties, and in this sense these landlords were not investment motivated. However, some of the formally operating sideline landlords had a deferred investment orientation, in that they often saw their property as a security for the future, some saying that future rental income would be, or would supplement, their pension.

It was clear that, whilst currently being formally operating sideline landlords, a few were actively pursuing a policy of building-up their portfolios to a point at which they would be able to earn their living solely from rental income. These embryonic business landlords were at an early stage of development from which several of the business landlords said they had first started. Indeed, one of the business landlords had started out by letting rooms in his own home.

Awareness of the role of the rent officer and the unreasonable rent rules

The diverse characteristics of private landlords was reflected in their knowledge of the rules governing Housing Benefit. For example, there were important differences between the respondents in terms of their awareness of the role of the rent officer and their knowledge of the rules on unreasonable rents. A substantial minority of sideline landlords, especially those operating on an informal basis, had no awareness of the existence of rent officers or their role in the Housing Benefit scheme. Even among those who did, the extent and accuracy of their knowledge varied. In contrast, all of the business landlords and letting agents knew that the rent officer had a role in the Housing Benefit scheme, which was commonly perceived to be that of checking that the rent being charged was not excessively high.

Compared with their knowledge of the rent officer, there was much more general awareness among sideline landlords that the rent might be considered too high by the

Housing Benefit office. But again, most of these landlords were rather hazy about both these aspects of the scheme and how they worked in practice. It was invariably interpreted as being to do with the level of the rent rather than the size of the accommodation. In contrast, all of the business landlords and letting agents were aware that it was possible for the rent to be restricted for Housing Benefit purposes. The extent and accuracy of this knowledge yet again varied but some of these respondents were very well informed about the rules, not just about high rents but also about the size criteria and, in a few cases, about rent increases. Not surprisingly, it was those business landlords and agents with a relatively high percentage of their tenants on Housing Benefit who were the most well informed about the rules.

Responding to rent restrictions

Sideline landlords had scarcely any actual experience of having tenants whose rent had been restricted by the Housing Benefit office. This was partly because of the fact that they had only one or a few lettings, but it was also seemed to be a function of the way in which they set their rent (this is discussed further below). Experience of rent restrictions was thus very largely confined to the business landlords and the managing agents.

How landlords and agents had responded to having had tenants whose rent had been restricted - or in the case of those with no experience, how they thought they might respond - varied considerably. Some landlords said the tenant had to make up the shortfall or leave, while others were prepared to negotiate a lower rent. In some cases which of these routes the landlord said they would take depended upon the size of the shortfall. Whereas they might let it go if the shortfall was small they would not do so if it were large. Some of the sideline landlords said they would not reduce the rent because they had costs that had to be covered.

One strategy which many of the business landlords and agents (and some of the formal sideline landlords) pursued was to insist that the tenant appealed against the restriction, an approach that apparently worked quite often. If the appeal failed, some said they would accept the shortfall while others (especially the managing agents) said the tenant would have to pay up or leave. Many agents made the point that, while the rent was negotiable at the beginning of a tenancy, once the tenant had agreed to it that was what they had to pay, whether the rent was subsequently restricted or not; not the least because it was a market rent and they saw no reason why the personal circumstances of the tenant - the fact that they were on Housing Benefit - should affect the rent being charged for the accommodation. If arrears developed, then many of the agents said they would deduct this from the tenant's deposit.

Setting the rent

The diverse characteristics of private landlords were also evident in the ways in which they set the rent for their lettings. Thus the sideline landlords, particularly those operating on a very informal basis, were much less 'market aware' than were the business landlords and letting agents. It was common for informal sideline landlords to ask the tenant what they thought the rent should be or what they had paid in their previous accommodation, in order to get some idea of what would be a 'reasonable' rent to charge. While some did consult the newspapers or lettings notice boards, other simply set the rent to cover their costs.

Some formal sideline landlords also set the rent to cover their costs. They tended to have a reserve price - which was based on their outgoings and in particular their mortgage repayments - below which they did not want to go. Some formal sideline landlords who were managing the property themselves consulted the newspapers and other sources to find out what other landlords were charging; and most of the landlords with a reserve rent checked it against the rents that others were charging. Landlords who used an agent, either to find a tenant or to manage the property, mostly relied on the advice of the agent to arrive at a figure for the rent.

Even those landlords who did consult sources of market information on rent levels did not always then set their rent at that amount. A number said they had pitched their rent deliberately below what they thought was the market level. This was not from some philanthropic purpose but was rather a strategy they employed to try and ensure that the property remained tenanted. They did not want the hassle, or the cost if they used an agent, of having to find a new tenant and nor did they want to lose rental income by having the property empty for a period while a new tenant was found.

In contrast to the sideline landlords, the business landlords were much more attuned to the state of the lettings market and generally more keen to set the rent at the market level. Even so, some of the business landlords also sought to set the rent at a bit below the market level in order to minimise the extent of tenant turnover.

Managing agents invariably said that they set the rent at the market level for the type, condition and location of the property. As they had considerable experience to draw on they were very attuned to what different properties would fetch in the lettings market. Nevertheless, agents reported that in some cases they were constrained by their landlord clients' requirements or instructions, though other landlords simply left it to them to decide upon the rent.

Housing Benefit and rent setting

The great majority of landlords and all of the agents who were interviewed reported that they took no account of the rent officer in deciding what rent to charge. In the case of those sideline landlords who were unaware of the rent officer, this was hardly surprising; but it was also true of most of the landlords who had heard of the rent officer and were aware that the rent could be restricted by the Housing Benefit office if it was considered to be too high.

Nevertheless, a minority of landlords did take the rent officer, or the fact that the Housing Benefit office could restrict high rents, into account when deciding what to charge. These landlords tended to have a relatively high proportion of tenants on Housing Benefit; since it was the decisions made by the rent officer and the Housing Benefit office which determined how much rent most or all of their tenants could afford to pay, taking them into account was a logical necessity.

The majority of landlords and agents said they charged the same rent to people on Housing Benefit as they did to those who were not. When asked this question, many of the landlords interpreted it to mean, do they charge a *lower* rent to Housing Benefit recipients. Invariably, the answer was 'No', they saw no reason, or could not afford, to discriminate between them and charge recipients a lower rent. In a few cases, however, the rent for people on Housing Benefit was lower than for people in work, mainly because the rent had been restricted; in a few others the respondent charged a higher price.

Letting strategies

Most landlords said they preferred not to let to people on Housing Benefit or did not have a preference either way. These findings accord with other recent research on private landlords and letting agents (eg, Kemp & Rhodes, 1994a, 1994b; Crook *et al*, 1995). Landlords who did not want to let to people on Housing Benefit tended to focus on two issues. The first was related to the undesirable image that landlords have of tenants on Housing Benefit. The second was related to difficulties encountered by landlords with the administration of the scheme.

Many landlords expressed concerns about how the Housing Benefit system operated. These most often mentioned delays in the processing of claims, and an inability to obtain information about the status of claims from Housing Benefit offices. Housing Benefit sent direct to the landlord, however, was viewed as an important positive aspect of the Housing Benefit system.

Whatever their preferences, most landlords were letting to people on Housing Benefit, some landlords and agents more than others. This was seen as inevitable because the rise in unemployment meant that many more tenants than previously were on Housing Benefit and the increase in the rental supply from people unable to sell their homes meant there was now more competition for tenants. However, at least one landlord was cutting out his present tenants who were on Housing Benefit and not letting any of his vacancies to such people because of rent restrictions.

Housing the homeless

The willingness of landlords to let their accommodation to tenants on Housing Benefit has implications for the acceptance of homeless households into the private rented sector on behalf of local authorities. If landlords had greater confidence in the administration of Housing Benefit, then this would facilitate easier access for people reliant on Housing Benefit, including homeless households.

The attitudes of landlords towards accepting homeless households on behalf of local authorities were mixed. Many business landlords and agents expressed interest in this proposal, and this was also true of a number of formal and informal sideline landlords. Several of the business landlords seemed quite keen on the idea and thought they might invest in additional properties, but they also mostly said it would only be feasible to do this if the local authority were to provide them with an improvement grant. Many of these landlords had expanded their portfolios by purchasing run down properties at low prices and then renovating them for letting.

Some formal and informal sideline landlords stated that they would not be prepared to accept homeless people, often because this would have meant sharing their own home with them. These dwelt upon what they often perceived as the undesirable image of homeless households. There was also the view that their property would be unsuitable for homeless families. Finally, some landlords who thought they might contemplate housing homeless people said they they would not house certain types of people, such as those with mental health problems.

Rent ceilings and pre-tenancy determinations

Many landlords were unsure about how the introduction of rent ceilings might affect their letting strategies or rent setting until the changes came into effect. It all depended upon how high or low the ceiling was. If the ceiling was too low, landlords would be reluctant to let to people on Housing Benefit; as a result, some said, it would unfairly penalise claimants and increase homelessness. But if it was set at a reasonable market level, then many respondents said they would have no problems with it and some (especially the managing agents) said they might look more favourably than they did at present upon prospective tenants who were on Housing Benefit.

Quite a few landlords thought that rent ceilings were a good idea because they would help to protect the public purse, but most of these respondents qualified this by stressing that the ceiling needed to be at a reasonable market level.

A number of landlords felt that both rent ceilings and pre-tenancy certificates would give them a useful indication of what they could expect from Housing Benefit; that is, it would act as a guideline rent. This would enable them to utilise a strategy of 'risk avoidance' if it was felt that Housing Benefit would not cover the amount of rent expected; if the rent ceiling or PTD was too low, they would know not to let their property to someone on Housing Benefit. This was particularly important for those landlords who required a specific rental income to cover mortgage or loan repayments.

Concluding remarks

It is clear that the Rachman stereotype that pervades much of the policy literature on private landlords - especially in relation to Housing Benefit - simply does not reflect the nature of private landlordism that was revealed in the interviews. As a recent qualitative study funded by the Department of the Environment (Thomas and Snape, 1995) and a quantitative survey funded by the Joseph Rowntree Foundation (Crook et al, 1995) have also found, private landlords have very diverse motives for letting their accommodation, many of which are non-commercial. Even among those landlords that were operating as a business, few gave the impression of seeking to exploit their customers but rather saw themselves as providing a service in return for which they hoped to make a reasonable living. Some did not see themselves as 'landlords' at all and were providing accommodation in order to help someone out or because they wanted companionship or help with their outgoings. Generally speaking, landlords had little desire to get rid of 'good' tenants - whom they mostly defined as people who paid the rent on time and looked after the property - but rather wanted them to stay and, indeed, in some cases charged less rent than they thought they could in order to keep them.

There was little evidence of landlords deliberating seeking, or being able, to take advantage of the Housing Benefit scheme. Where landlords or agents were very knowledgeable about the scheme or were influenced by the rent officer, this was usually because most of their tenants were on Housing Benefit and they consequently had little choice but to take the rent officer into account. It was apparent, however, that in some cases, the existence of the rent officer and the rules on restrictions in eligible rents were a constraining influence on the rents which landlords felt able to charge. Moreover one of the managing agents did seek to charge recipients a higher rent than people in work. In contrast, landlords and agents who let accommodation much less often to people on Housing Benefit had relatively little knowledge of the scheme and had no need to adjust their behaviour to take into account the rent officer service or the local authority Housing Benefit office.

So far as tenant selection is concerned, the fact that a tenant was on Housing Benefit was more likely to be a cause of concern than an opportunity to be exploited, simply because taking on a recipient was felt to increase the risks of letting. The idea of pre-tenancy determinations was welcomed by most landlords precisely because it would help to reduce for them the risk of letting accommodation to a Housing Benefit recipient only to find that, when their entitlement was determined, they could not afford the accommodation. Even so, the delays in the processing of claims, the problems of overpaid benefit, tenants leaving before their benefit claim was processed, and the perceived lack of helpfulness of some Housing Benefit offices, were all factors which made letting accommodation to recipients a risky business which many landlords would prefer to be without.

References

Audit Commission (1993) *Remote Control: The National Administration of Housing Benefit*, London: HMSO.

Blake, J. (1994) 'The agents of change', *Roof*, 19 (4), July and August, pp26-29.

Crook, A.D.H., Hughes, J. and Kemp, P.A. (1995) *The Supply of Privately Rented Homes*, York: Joseph Rowntree Foundation.

Department of the Environment (1994) *Access to Local Authority and Housing Association Tenancies*, London: Department of the Environment.

Department of the Environment (1995) *Rent Officer Statistics*, London: Government Statistical Service.

Department of Social Security (1995) *Memorandum to the Social Security Advisory Committee: Housing Benefit Changes for Private Sector Tenants*, London: Department of Social Security.

Downs, D., Holmans, A. and Small, H. (1994) *Trends in the Size of the Private Rented Sector in England*, London: HMSO.

Jenn, M. (1994) *Housing Homeless People in the Private Rented Sector*, Manchester: Churches National Housing Coalition.

Kemp, P.A. (1990) 'Deregulation, markets and the 1988 Housing Act', *Social Policy and Administration*, 24 (2), August, pp145-155.

Kemp, P.A. and McLaverty, P. (1993a) *Unreasonable Rents and Housing Benefit*, Centre for Housing Policy Discussion Paper no. 2, York: University of York.

Kemp, P.A. and McLaverty, P. (1993b) *Rent Officers and Housing Benefit*, Centre for Housing Policy Discussion Paper no. 3, York: University of York.

Kemp, P.A. and McLaverty, P. (1995) *Private Tenants and Restrictions in Rent for Housing Benefit*, Centre for Housing Policy, York: University of York.

Kemp, P.A., Oldman, C., Rugg, J. and Williams, T. (1994) *The Effects of Benefit on Housing Decisions*, London: HMSO.

Kemp, P.A. and Rhodes, D. (1994a) *The Lower End of the Private Rented Sector*, Edinburgh: Scottish Homes.

Kemp, P.A. and Rhodes, D. (1994b) *Private Landlords in Scotland*, Edinburgh: Scottish Homes.

London Housing Unit (1994) *The Cost of the Government's Homelessness Proposals*, London: London Housing Unit.

Lilley, P. (1994) 'Social Security Statement', *Hansard*, 30 November.

Miller, K. (1994) 'Finding new safety nets', *Roof*, 19 (4), July and August, pp38-41.

NACAB (1990) *Market Failure: Low Income Households and the Private Rented Sector*, London: National Association of Citizens' Advice Bureaux.

NACAB (1991) *System Overload: The Housing Benefit System in Crisis*, London: National Association of Citizens' Advice Bureaux.

Randall, G. and Brown, S. (1994) *Private Renting for Single Homeless People: An Evaluation of a Pilot Rent Deposit Fund*, London: HMSO.

Sharp, C. (1991) *Problems Assured!*, London: SHAC.

Thomas, A.D. and Hedges, A. (1986) *The 1985 Physical and Social Survey of HMO's in England and Wales*, London: HMSO.

Thomas, A. and Snape, D. (1994) *In from the Cold - Working with the Private Landlord*, London: Department of the Environment.

Timmins, N. (1994) 'landlords 'costing taxpayers billions', *Independent*, 3 August.

Zebedee, J. And Ward, M. (1995) *Guide to Housing Benefit and Council Tax Benefit 1995/96*, London: Chartered Institute of Housing and Shelter.